God, Why Don't You Hear Their Prayer?

Making a difference in Spite of Injustice

Tom Eggum &
Rachel Eggum-Cinader

Unless otherwise indicated, Bible quotations are taken from the
New International Version (NIV) of the Bible. Copyright 1973, 1978, 1984
by the International Bible Society. All rights reserved. Used by permission.

Scripture quotations marked MSG are taken from The Message. Copyright
by Eugene H. Peterson, 1993, 1994, 1995. Used by permission of
NavPress Publishing Group.

Scripture quotations marked NLT are taken from the Holy Bible, New Living
Translation, copyright 1996, 2004. Used by permission of Tyndale House
Publishers, Inc., Wheaton, Illinois 60189. All rights reserved.

Published by
VMI PUBLISHERS
Sisters, Oregon
www.vmipublishers.com

ISBN: 1-933204-53-2
ISBN 13: 978-1-933204-53-6
Library of Congress Control Number: 2007942424

Printed in the USA.

Cover design by Joe Bailen

FOR MORE INFORMATION about future international trips, orphan sponsorship
or donation opportunities, we invite you to visit our website at
www.hope4kidsinternational.org.
Tom and/or Rachel are available for speaking at mission events, churches or
civic organizations. To contact them, please email
Tom@hope4kidsinternational.org.

Table of Contents

Dedication

We would like to dedicate this book to the memory of our parents who modeled reaching out to the poor and the outcasts of society. To our dad for his great gift of compassion and to our mom who passed on her free spirit, sense of adventure and her love of writing. Both had unwavering faith in God even when not all was right in their world. We are grateful for their love and the standards they exemplified.

Tom and Rachel

Chapter One

God, Where Are You?

Thirty-two years of traveling the world as the founding president of Hope4Kids International did not prepare me for what I saw in Africa. A friend talked me into speaking at a conference in a village outside of Tororo, Uganda. Reluctantly I went, knowing I would meet destitute people. Our ministry was already involved in so many other projects; we were operating in the red, therefore my board of directors warned me not to commit to anything.

The village church was a dilapidated, wooden structure that should have been condemned. It leaned dangerously. As people jumped, clapped and shouted to the Lord, I feared the building would collapse. Children joined in the worship with as much frenzy as the adults. Some of the children had bloated bellies from parasites and malnourishment; some were coughing, while many had runny noses.

I continued observing the children as their worship shifted from dancing to dropping to their knees. Tears splashed down their cheeks and onto the floor, forming little puddles in the dirt. Their hands were raised high. Completely focused on Him, they did not seem to notice the flies crawling over their open sores.

In the village and surrounding area were thousands of orphans. Families who could not afford to feed their own children were forced to take in children of their sisters, daughters, cousins, and co-wives who had died of AIDS.

The pastor lived in a shack of crude boards with large gaps. His house was virtually the size of my hotel bathroom yet he had just taken in two more children. I asked, "Pastor, with all the people living in your home how could you take in more?"

"When we lie down on the floor to sleep at night, there is space for two more."

To find clean water people walked two to three miles one way and hauled home as much as they could carry. Many collected contaminated water from streams and puddles close by and were dying from dysentery after consuming it. I learned dysentery was the number three killer in this area, while malaria was number one and measles was number two. AIDS was fourth. My lip trembled when I realized their top three fatal diseases were easily treated. How many people could be saved if medicine were available? If there were a clinic, people could receive treatment and be educated about disease prevention. What if a well were dug? How many lives could be redeemed?

I visited a public hospital and was appalled to see the conditions were primitive, filthy, and overcrowded. Medicine was scarce to non-existent. The corrupt medical system left the hospital as only a place to come die.

The children's wards are so congested that unless a child needs to be connected to an IV he is forced to stay outside during the daytime. Some lie on reed mats while others try to rest on the sidewalk or in the dirt. Family members come to care for them and are responsible for bringing food, soap, a basin and anything else the patient needs. If a patient needs any kind of treatment from an aspirin to an injection to a clean dressing, the family member must bribe the nurse. If they have no money the patient receives no treatment. If they do not receive treatment, they die.

I moved through the wards of the local hospital and cried out to God as I saw people in such weakened conditions they could only manage a nod when I asked if I could pray for them. I have seen children with wide, frightened eyes staring at their mothers as if silently begging them not to die.

In the village a beautiful woman, Grace, and her son brought me a chicken and eggs. Grace knelt before me presenting them to me in thanks for my coming to Africa. The next day I was visiting orphans in their huts and Grace's son came running. "Mr. Tom. Come quickly. My mother is sick." I followed him into their little one-room hut and waited for my eyes to adjust to the darkness. There was no electricity and the only light came through the open doorway. Grace was lying on a reed mat on the dirt floor so weakened by AIDS she could not rise. She wanted prayer. I choked back tears as I knelt next to her and pleaded with God to heal her body. Afterward I glanced around her hut and realized she had given me a large portion of her wealth when she gave me the chicken and eggs.

I thought about the widow in the New Testament. Jesus and his disciples were at the temple. Jesus sat down opposite the place where the offerings were put and watched the crowd putting their money into the temple treasury. Many rich people threw in large amounts. But a poor widow came and put in two very small copper coins, worth only a fraction of a penny. Calling his disciples to him, Jesus said, "I tell you the truth, this poor widow has put more into the treasury than all the others. They all gave out of their wealth; but she, out of her poverty, put in everything—all she had to live on." (Mark 12:41-44)

There are a number of widows in Uganda. Thirty-seven-year-old Rukia's husband died of AIDS but not before infecting her. Devastated, sick, and with no means to care for herself and her three boys, Rukia was cast out from her husband's family home the day he was buried. A friend took pity on her and invited her and the boys to share her one-room hut but soon realized she could not afford to accommodate them and told Rukia they would have to move out.

Rukia decided to send her boys back to her husband's family. Surely they would take care of their own. When the boys arrived, their father's family asked them to sit and wait while they prepared a meal for them.

They were hungry and waited eagerly for the spread that would quiet the rumblings in their stomachs. A neighbor happened by and overheard the family discussing how much rat poisoning they should put into the food in order to kill the boys. She rushed to their rescue and helped them escape, returning them to Rukia.

Sadly Rukia contemplated if it would have been better had the boys eaten the poison. Then she could kill herself and it would all be over. Surely God had forgotten her.

I heard stories of desperate people abandoning their children. Babies have been found in trash heaps and latrines. One baby was fished out of a ninety foot latrine and had multiple problems from breathing in all the waste. Girls find themselves alone with a baby after their boyfriends have run off, or they have been raped. Scared and having no means to raise a baby, often they will take the baby to the hospital claiming he is sick, give a fictitious name and disappear.

Very young children are on their own in the bush and in the streets. It is not uncommon to see a two-year-old boy alone in the bush collecting firewood or a four-year-old girl with a baby strapped to her back. Babies caring for babies…

I wondered how many years will it take to educate people on the issue of AIDS. Between widespread polygamy and truckers spreading AIDS throughout Africa, the task seems daunting. I saw trucks lined up at the local cement factory and women standing next to them waiting to prostitute themselves. Many carried babies on their backs.

There are still so many myths surrounding AIDS. Men believe having sex with a virgin rids them of AIDS thus causing young girls to not only be violated but also infected. It is a vicious cycle…poverty, lack of education and disease.

Back at the hotel that night I could not sleep. I contemplated what Grace's life must be like and wondered how she fed her children. I cried when I thought of all the Rukias with their unwanted children. I wondered how I could be so blessed and have all I want to eat while children slowly starve here in Africa. In the States I live the American dream while in the middle of the jungle lives a woman with nothing. She gave away all she had. Images of the many I had seen suffering from extreme poverty kept playing through my mind. I was angry at the disease I had seen. I ached for all those orphans.

Falling to my knees next to my bed I cried out: "God! Don't You hear their prayers? These people love You more than I ever could. At home I pray for stupid things like a close parking spot. Here in the middle of Africa are the most joyful, beautiful people on the planet, and they have nothing. Children are dying daily. Parents are succumbing to AIDS, leaving thousands of orphans, yet they worship enthusiastically and joyfully before You. Why? Where are You? Why don't You hear their prayer?"

Chapter Two

Created for His Purpose

Sobbing, I rested my forehead on the edge of the bed. When I was depleted I quietly remained there. In the stillness I sensed God speaking. "I have heard their prayer. That's why you're here."

"Me?" I leaped to my feet. "My budget is in the red. The needs are overwhelming. What can I do? I am already overcommitted. This is a real crisis!"

I discerned God saying He had already prepared the hearts of giving people in the States. If I were to tell them what I had seen, they would respond.

I went home and spoke in churches, showing photos and telling the heartbreaking stories of children dying of treatable diseases. I told of the need for a clinic stocked with medicine. I talked of the filthy water conditions. I reported on the church, the living conditions of the people, and the thousands of orphaned children.

People responded as never before. The first weekend I received checks from two individuals to cover the cost of building a clinic, and my board of directors funded a well. Within the first two weeks, 120 orphans were sponsored. When I showed my pastor, Dr. Don Wilson of Christ's Church of the Valley in Phoenix, pictures of the humble Ugandan church, he put them on an overhead and asked our congregation, "Is it right for us to be moving into a fourteen million dollar complex when our brothers and sisters in Uganda are worshiping in this?" An offering at the door brought enough money to build a spacious church for the Ugandans.

I realized a long time ago the call on my life was to do more than speak about Jesus. When I began meeting the suffering around the world, I knew I would have to try to meet some of their basic needs in order to open their eyes to a loving God.

My parents modeled this behavior in reaching out to the hurting after God transformed their lives. Before I was born my parents lived a crazy, party life. My dad was an alcoholic and my mom kept marrying the wrong kind of husbands. My three older sisters were often left alone while my parents hung out at the local bar.

Mom sometimes listened to a radio Bible teacher, John D. Jess. When he once announced he was going to speak at a church in a nearby town, somehow Mom talked Dad into going.

They enjoyed the service and met the minister who began dropping by their home each week to share how Jesus loved and died for them. Other church members brought ice cream and kept my sisters company on nights they were alone. Because a few people reached out in love, one day my parents said yes to Jesus.

Enthusiastic to live for the Lord, my parents believed it necessary to follow a list of stern rules. People in our small town placed bets on how long this religion would last. The transformation was a shock to my older sisters who had been free to go to the movies or roam the streets while my parents were out drinking. Suddenly they were forced to go to church on Sunday morning and on Sunday and Thursday evenings. Thrust into an uncompromising lifestyle, they no longer were allowed to go to movies or dances and were expected to join my parents each evening for Bible reading and prayer.

My dad was adamant about tithing. With his meager income, it was a stretch to provide for a family of nine and to give his first ten percent to the church, but we always had something to eat and good pairs of shoes. Friends and church members gave us hand-me-down clothing. Martha Harding, a school friend, was a little older than my two younger sisters. She gave them her dresses as she outgrew them. In our small school the other kids always recognized them and would ask my sisters, "Is that Martha Harding's dress?"

Our church frequently hosted visiting missionaries, who showed slides and displayed jewelry, baskets, traditional clothing and maps in an effort to bring their world to ours. Those I remember most were from Africa. We would laugh nervously at the scantily clad people. Topless women wore heavy, bright necklaces and thick earrings made of bones, teeth and stones while others had rings in their noses. The men stood soberly still in their loin cloths.

A missionary couple awoke their first morning in an African village to find a group gathered outside their bedroom window, crowding and shoving one another as they watched the white missionaries sleep.

We would watch and listen in wonder. Here we were in a small town in rural Iowa hearing stories that had us gripping the edges of our seats.

One missionary was approached by the village chief, who hated his teachings on Jesus. The chief handed him an egg. "If your God is real, throw this egg against the wall. If it bounces without breaking I will believe. If it breaks your God is dead and so are you."

The missionary tried to explain the Bible says do not tempt God, but the chief was unyielding. Knowing his life was on the line, the missionary breathed a plea to God and threw the egg against the wall. To his astonishment and to those around him the egg bounced like a rubber ball. The chief grabbed the egg and handed it to him once more. "Do it again."

Oh no, this is really tempting God. The missionary glanced at the relentless chief, prayed and threw the egg a second time. Again it bounced like a rubber ball. The chief snatched up the egg and flung it. Everyone silently stared as it splattered and oozed down the wall. The village chief, along with many who had witnessed the miracle, knelt to accept Christ.

Mom and Dad welcomed missionaries into our home. Mom scraped together the finest meal she could muster up and graciously shared what we had. Each month Dad sent a check of ten to fifteen dollars toward their support. Mom ordered a little plastic record player with a crank on top where you placed your finger and manually turned the turntable. We had so much fun with it until she boxed it up along with a stack of Christian records and sent it to missionaries who had no electricity.

At the edge of our little town was a substantial potato farm. Every year Mexican migrant workers arrived to work the fields, and the man who owned the farm provided housing for them in a migrant camp. The camp had a number of shacks with no running water or electricity, forcing the residents to share a community well and an outhouse. The migrant workers were carefree as they ran in and out of one another's houses, sharing everything from food to clothes to laughter. They did not seem to mind that they were poor. I do not know if they even realized it. I found myself envying them with their great sense of community.

As a mechanic my dad was called upon to fix broken machinery at the potato farm. He and the migrant workers became friends and our family regularly visited their camp. Dad wanted everyone to know Jesus, so each Sunday he dropped us off early at Sunday school and headed to the migrant camp where he crammed as many people into his car as possible and brought them to church. Sometimes he had to make two trips. Soon many of the migrant workers were attending and since most of the adults did not speak English, our little church found a Christian Spanish teacher willing to hold Spanish services. We attended as well since Dad picked up those who did not have a ride and Mom played the piano. Rachel has always loved Spanish and knew how to pronounce the words even though she did not know their meaning. She can still sing "En la Cruz" at the top of her lungs.

Dad, a true friend to the migrant workers, repaired their cars and charged them as little as he dared. Once a used car dealer cheated one of the men by overcharging for a worthless car and somehow Dad got involved. There was a big discussion in our front yard with the salesman and a number of migrant workers. The salesman did make it right after an afternoon of arguing and threats from my dad. The migrant workers all trusted Dad after that and brought many of their problems to him. Whenever they came he tried to help and then pointed them to Jesus.

My parents set a first-rate example in reaching out to others. They gave despite the fact they had so little and counted it a privilege. They never forgot the life from which Christ had rescued them and desired to constantly show that same mercy to others. Both are now at home with our Heavenly Father.

When my mom died in 2000, my sister Joan was given the chore of going through all of Mom's paperwork. She found a letter Mom had written to John D. Jess shortly after I was born when she was still questioning Christianity. After asking many questions she wrote:

One last thing. Who was it that brought her son to Elijah and asked him to raise him in the ministry? I brought my baby son to your service last night. Above all my thoughts I thought "Wouldn't it be wonderful if John D. Jess could teach my son in the ways of God, so that he could carry on God's work." This summer when I first saw the light, I was expecting this baby; I wanted a son so badly after having three daughters that I prayed that if God would give me a son I would guide him into ministry. A vision came to me that this child would become a saver of souls and at his birth I felt, "Thank God." The little fellow was so tiny, so weak that for the first few weeks there was some doubt if he would make it. But I did not give up hope. I felt, "I've dedicated this child to the Lord's work. He will let him live." Now he is progressing beautifully and I shall not go back on my word— I shall be proud to see him bringing the people back to God.

Tears clouded my eyes as I read the mind-blowing letter. I marveled that I had never heard this testimony. Glancing back at my teen years, I thought how her heart must have broken when she saw the rebellion in me. She was certain God had heard her prayer. I wondered if her faith faltered. I wondered how many nights she and Dad spent on their knees crying out to God on my behalf. I wondered if she ever reflected on her vision when she saw me return to the Lord and preach all over the world. I wondered why she never told me.

Now and again I stop to thank God for my parents' legacy, for the love they showed to the hurting and for the evangelists and missionaries who depended upon the meager but faithfully given money my parents donated toward their ministries.

This is how we know what love is: Jesus Christ laid down his life for us. And we ought to lay down our lives for our brothers. If anyone has material possessions and sees his brother in need but has no pity on him, how can the love of God be in him? Dear children, let us not love with words or tongue, but with actions and in truth. (1 John 3:16-18)

My parents pointed us toward eternal life with Christ and showed us how to live abundantly serving Him and to attain a servant's heart by helping others. I marvel that they did not use their poverty as an excuse to hold back but constantly believed God would supply their needs as they cared for the needs of others.

William Booth, founder of the Salvation Army, said:

But what is the use of preaching the Gospel to men whose whole attention is concentrated upon a mad, desperate struggle to keep themselves alive? You might as well give a tract to a shipwrecked sailor who is battling with the surf which has drowned his comrades and threatens to drown him. He will not listen to you. Nay, he cannot hear you any more than a man whose head is underwater can listen to a sermon. The first thing to do is to get him at least a footing on firm ground, and to give him room to live. Then you may have a chance . . . And you will have all the better opportunity to find a way to his heart, if he comes to know that it was you who pulled him out of the horrible pit and the miry clay in which he was sinking to perdition.[1]

The Salvation Army's principles and the example of my parents helped form the foundation of Hope4Kids International as we strive to bring the message of hope through four paths:

1. We bring hope through **health**. Team members hand-carry tens of thousands of dollars worth of medicine. Our medical people partner with local medical personnel and provide free medical and dental clinics in underprivileged neighborhoods and villages. In Uganda and Peru we have built and staffed new medical clinics as well as a hospital in Uganda.

2. We provide hope through **joy**. We believe kids should be able to laugh and play. We carry soccer balls, beanie babies, baseballs, toys and games. Whenever we see kids we play, put on puppet shows, and sing and dance with them, we come across kids who are sick, hurting, abused and abandoned. If they can laugh for a few minutes then those are a few moments that they do not hurt. We have been told by hospital staff that they have seen a positive turn in the health of very sick children as they sing our songs and perform puppet shows of their own, using their socks as puppets, for weeks after we have gone.

3. We provide hope through **dignity**. We pass out food and clothing and hand out blankets to the homeless. We fix teeth. Beauticians and manicurists do makeovers on women, giving new life to people who have little self-esteem. We put shoes on the feet of children who have none and watch their new confidence as they strut in what is often their first pair of new shoes. When we see a need, we try to meet it in order to bring value to a life.

4. We provide hope through **love**. As we share the love of Christ through our actions and words, we want people to know God is merciful and that He is waiting with His arms wide open. Because of Christ's boundless mercy toward us, we long to demonstrate that mercy to others.

A director of a Romanian orphanage told us, "Many groups have come to tell about Jesus, but your group shows us Jesus by your actions and your gifts." I believe we are far more effective in sharing the gospel by living like Jesus than just telling people the gospel. William Booth instructed his workers, "When you give a gospel tract to a hungry man, wrap it up in a sandwich!" He would add, "Love spoken can easily be turned away, but love demonstrated will last for a lifetime."² When we are asked why we do what we do, we tell of God sending His Son Jesus and how He showed His incredible love and mercy toward us by dying on the cross for our sins. We tell how Jesus was attracted to the wounded, the poor and the forgotten, and we are trying to model His love and mercy. It is miraculous how placing a pair of shoes on a child impacts that life. Once in Romania our team was eating at a pizza parlor. Some team members noticed three ragged, preteen street boys standing outside in their bare feet. They grabbed an interpreter and some shoes and rushed outside. The faces of the boys radiated with pride and dignity when the women knelt and placed new shoes on their feet. One year later when I led another team to Romania, Debbi, one of the women, returned with us. We were doing an outreach to street kids who were living in a cave outside of town. A local pastor partnered with us and arrived with a group of young boys. One of them looked at Debbi and said, "Gabby (his nickname for her), I remember you from last year. You put shoes on my feet. It changed my life." After Debbi had given him shoes her translator took him home to live with her. He accepted Christ and was now working with the pastor reaching out to other street kids.

The first time Rachel went to Uganda, she met Isaac who had no shoes. Our team brought shoes to distribute to the orphans and Isaac sat quietly by, knowing he would not receive any because he was not an orphan. His longing turned to joy when Rachel took him aside and gifted him with a pair of shoes he had been eyeing.

When Rachel returned to Uganda six months later and disembarked from our bus, Isaac's father was waiting for her. He could not wait to tell her his news. "My wife had a baby girl last month. Isaac insisted that we name her Rachel, 'because,' as Isaac said, 'Rachel gave me shoes.'"

Howard Thurman, a Black civil rights leader, is often quoted as saying: "Don't ask yourself what the world needs. Ask yourself what makes you come alive and go do that. Because what the world needs is people who have come alive."[3] God has designed us for the purpose of living this life to the fullest. "The thief comes only to steal and kill and destroy; I have come that they may have life, and have it to the full." (John 10:10)

Why is it some of the people who are the least fulfilled are those who have been so successful in the eyes of the world? They have accumulated many things in life, but they are left unsatisfied and lack significance. They do not feel alive!

Solomon, the richest man ever, said:

I denied myself nothing my eyes desired; I refused my heart no pleasure. My heart took delight in all my work, and this was the reward for all my labor. Yet when I surveyed all that my hands had done and what I had toiled to achieve, everything was meaningless, a chasing after the wind; nothing was gained under the sun. (Ecclesiastes 2:10-11)

I believe the purpose of followers of Jesus Christ should be clear. God has given each of us gifts and talents according to His design. We are to passionately use these gifts and opportunities to the best of our abilities.

We have different gifts, according to the grace given us. If a man's gift is prophesying, let him use it in proportion to his faith. If it is serving, let him serve; if it is teaching, let him teach; if it is encouraging, let him encourage; if it is contributing to the needs of others, let him give generously; if it is leadership, let him govern diligently; if it is showing mercy, let him do it cheerfully. (Romans 12:6-8).

After my night of wrestling with God in my Ugandan hotel room, I emerged with a stronger sense of God's purpose. Nothing has grabbed my heart nor cried out to me more loudly and passionately as this. I constantly think about our projects in Uganda. I dream about them. I look at every angle to make a difference in the lives of these amazing people.

Rachel's husband Robert is seventy-one and has been to Uganda nine times within three years. A retired electrician, he has trained four young Ugandan men in electrical work. These young men who had nothing now are becoming skilled tradesmen. Robert says he worked fifty years to train for what God really wanted him to do. While in Uganda, Robert dreams all night long—often with his eyes wide open. At breakfast he waves his arms and talks excitedly about a new idea he has to improve the lives of the Ugandans. He has found and is living out God's purpose in his life.

Do you know that passion? Have you found your purpose? I encourage you to be faithful to the Lord in whatever He has called you to do. It is a joy and celebration when you can give and bring hope to the world through the gifts God has given you.

…On the day he comes to be glorified in his holy people and to be marveled at among all those who have believed. This includes you, because you believed our testimony to you. With this in mind, we constantly pray for you, that our God may count you worthy of his calling, and that by his power he may fulfill every good purpose of yours and every act prompted by your faith. We pray this so that the name of our Lord Jesus may be glorified in you, and you in him, according to the grace of our God and the Lord Jesus Christ." (2 Thessalonians 1:10-12)

Our purpose as Christians is to bring hope to those in need. Our message is one of victory. This is a critical time to influence the society in which we live. We need to decide if we are going to run and hide or get involved. We are this world's only hope.

We, who have been left with the great commission to go into the entire world, know the giver of life, the One who promises hope eternal!

In 1885 William Booth challenged the Salvationists:

What are you living for? What is the deep secret purpose that controls and fashions your existence? What do you eat and drink for? What is the end of your marrying and giving in marriage— your money-making and toilings and plannings? Is it the salvation of souls, the overthrow of the kingdom of evil, and the setting up of the Kingdom of God? Have you the assurance that the ruling passion of your life is the same as that which brought Christ to the manger, led Him to fight the foul fiend of hell in the wilderness, bore Him onward upon the back of suffering and tears and ignoring the baptism of blood, bore Him through Gethsemane, nailed Him to the Cross of Calvary, and enabled Him in triumph to open the gate of the Kingdom? Is that what you are living for? If not, you may be religious—a very proper person amongst religionists—but I don't see how you can be a Christian.[4]

Chapter Three

Mission Africa

As I go through my daily routine something keeps yanking at my thoughts, my heart and my spirit. When I lie down to sleep, I dream of orphans, of mothers struggling to survive AIDS, of fathers trying to provide for their families in a poverty stricken land. I dream of a little village outside of Tororo, Uganda where people live in mud huts with no electricity and have to carry heavy pails of water on their heads as they trudge home from the community well. I see visions of them cooking a meager meal of greens, vegetables or porridge over a little campfire. I imagine cheery, grimy little kids in tattered clothing stirring the earth with their bare feet and waiting for a little bit to eat before they lie down to sleep.

Sometimes I awaken during the night and go to the refrigerator. I dig around for something to eat and think about my friends in Uganda and wonder what they do when they wake up hungry. They do not have a refrigerator stocked with their favorite foods from Costco. They can not throw a pizza into an oven or heat leftovers in a microwave and there are no snacks. If they are hungry they wait. That does not mean they will eat. We visited a school and were told that only 200 of the 1000 kids can afford lunch, and of those 800 who do not eat lunch a great number may not have dinner when they get home.

When I nestle into our warm comfy bed and adjust my fluffy feather pillow, visions of those dirty little kids in torn clothes pop up again. Are they warm? Are they comfortable? Did they eat tonight? I lie back and pull our extra thick comforter up under my chin. I think about kids sleeping on dirt floors sharing a ragged blanket with other kids. Those in our orphan program have been given mattresses, so I know there are certain kids sleeping on mattresses tonight even though they are probably sharing with three or more other kids. Maybe they will keep one another warm. The twin-sized mattresses we purchase in Uganda are not pillow topped or sleep numbered. They are three or four inches thick of foam covered with cheap plastic. The mattress is placed on the dirt floor at night and as many family members as can crowd together and lie down to sleep. If they are blessed they have two to place side-by-side. I think about my two young children and how they had a hot meal, a warm bath and dressed in their cute, clean pajamas were tucked between downy soft sheets on their spongy beds.

Once when Rachel mentioned tucking kids into bed, Jane, a Ugandan, asked, "What is that?"

Rachel explained how we escort our children to bed, read them a story and pray with them before kissing them goodnight and pulling the covers snugly around them.

Jane put one hand on her ample hip and stared at Rachel shaking her head in disbelief. "I have never done that or heard of anyone doing that!"

"How do you put your kids to bed?"

"We say, 'Go to bed.'"

I close my eyes and try to turn off my mind. I can not seem to find the switch as thoughts of Cadija sneak across the threshold. Rachel is working on a book about the women of Uganda so Jane set up interviews for her with some of the oldest widows she could find. They arrived at Cadija's home to find this 120-year-old lame woman crawling around outside her mud hut trying to replace mud that had caved in during heavy rains. Outside drying in the sun were all her belongings, which consisted of a pile of filthy rags, a brittle, broken plastic wash basin and a small saucepan with a few wilted greens floating in an unrecognizable liquid.

Neighbors said Cadija bunches up the rags every night and fashions them into a bed. She fends for herself by crawling around the bush searching for firewood and something to eat. They said they carry water from the well but if Cadija isn't there and they leave it by her door, others come by and steal it. Her skin was like an alligator and her fingernails and toenails were long, yellow, curled and dirt encrusted.

Cadija greeted the two women with a wide toothless smile and sat back to enjoy a visit. "In the old days we couldn't just stop and talk like this. There was too much work to do."

Jane asked, "Ja Ja (Grandma), do your eyes still see?"

"Yes."

"Do you see my friend?"

"Yes. I see Mzungu (white person)."

"Have you had anything to eat today?"

"I don't have any water and no one to get it for me."

Immediately the man who escorted the women ran to the well and filled two buckets with water. Jane showed Cadija the gifts they had brought of rice, soap, biscuits, sugar, and beans along with new sheets and a blanket. Cadija raised her hands and gave glory to God over and over. Jane wrapped a sheet around her and she sat laughing in luxury while repeatedly listing off the items and saying she could not believe someone would give her all those things. Jane pressed a bill of 10,000 shillings (5.40 in US dollars) into her hands as they prayed for her and left. They commissioned a neighbor to re-mud her house and promised one another they would buy Cadija a mattress and return the next week.

The next week Rachel and Jane returned along with other women from the States, carrying a mattress for Cadija. A normally vocal Cadija sat in silent awe upon her new mattress. The Americans stood still watching and pondering how a person reaches the age of 120 without ever sleeping on a mattress. They encouraged Cadija to lie down which she quickly did and collapsed in contented surrender. Those watching dabbed their eyes and wondered why their lives were so blessed. Pointing to a strip of cloth knotted at her waist Cadija said a neighbor had taken her shillings to buy supplies and her change was secured in the knot. She said she never takes off the belt even when she sleeps. The money she guarded so carefully amounted to a little over two dollars.

On one of Rachel's numerous return visits, she and her team brought tea and donuts. Cadija was sitting outside her hut waiting for her visitors and cried in jubilation when she saw them. She showed them her mattress and how she had covered it with cloths to protect it. It looked new! The team looked around at the walls and realized Cadija's house would crumble soon. Jane pointed out holes where rats gnawed through. The grass roof was in terrible shape and she would get wet when the rains came.

The team presented Cadija with a new purple basin and a beautiful pink purse with the words Faith, Hope and Love imprinted upon it. She opened the purse which was jammed with gifts. Laughing she warned: "No one had better try to steal these from me. If you are the person who paid for it, you can come and get it. But if you didn't pay...leave it alone!"

Surrounded by her gifts she joked, "Now I need a new house to put these beautiful things in."

Rachel handed her a cup of hot green tea and everyone watched her down it quickly. "Did you like it?"

"Have I not drunk it all?"

When Cadija opened the packages of food, she immediately crawled into her hut and started cooking. Realizing the visit was over the team called "Bye". Cadija called "Bye" over her shoulder and happily stirred her porridge.

Later Rachel asked Robert, "Do you think you could put a team together to build Cadija a new mud hut? Would the Americans think that would be something fun?"

Robert gathered his Ugandan friends, and together with the team from the States they built a new hut within three days. Cadija sat in the doorway of her old hut watching and marveling that someone would build a home for her and not ask for anything in return. She talked and laughed with neighbors as they stopped by to congratulate her.

Colleen Volk from Seattle decided it was time to ask Cadija if she wanted to accept Christ. Kneeling next to Cadija Colleen said, "God healed me from cancer so I could come here and lead you to Christ."

Cadija responded: "Everyone has forgotten me. Yet you people keep coming back bringing me gifts and food. You brought me tea. You bought me rice. People who are not even from my tribe are building me a new house. I know it is because of Jesus and I want to know Jesus too."

As soon as they prayed Cadija announced: "I'm saved! I don't want my Muslim name anymore! I am now Wazemba."

That night while she slept Cadija's (or should I say Wazemba's) old hut collapsed. The neighbors heard her cries and rushed to pull her from the rubble. She was unharmed and in high spirits because she would be moving into her new hut the next day.

I roll over to my side. Maybe I can sleep now. I have heard so many stories in Uganda it is difficult to not dwell on them.

On my first trip to Uganda, I met two teenage sisters living alone in a small wooden shack near the cement factory. Like so many orphans their parents had surrendered to AIDS, leaving the girls to find their own way in life. Beatrice supported the two by designing and sewing garments on a treadle sewing machine in a tiny shop. She earned enough to support them and to pay for her sister Sophie's school fees. As I connected with these two girls, I told them I would be their daddy now. I enrolled Beatrice in school and searched for an apartment in a safer area. The men from the cement factory would frequently be drunk, and I feared the girls were in jeopardy of being violated, and that had happened too many times in their short lives already, so I found a home for them next to the man Beatrice worked for. He and his wife became the girls' unofficial guardians. The girls were happy to have a daddy and were anxious to meet Mommy Sarah. They were so proud of their new home with a cement floor and a light bulb! There was a community outhouse and a bathing house where they could carry a basin of water and bathe in privacy within a wooden structure. I paid their rent, purchased food and supplies and a large pad-lock. When I returned to the States, they wailed in distress and begged me not to go.

Sophie and Beatrice are excellent students and love to study. Sophie wants to be a doctor and quips, "The roots of education are bitter but the fruit is sweet."

One afternoon while in Uganda I called to Robert and Rachel and asked if they wanted to go see their nieces. Immediately they left their tasks and walked the hot, dusty path with me. Delighted to see us, the girls set their books aside and sent a neighbor for sodas. We three sat together on a wooden love seat while Beatrice pulled back a curtain and sat on the bed. Sophie brought in a little wooden stool for herself and sipped her orange soda through a straw. "When I was a little girl my mommy and daddy died. I missed them so much and was so angry with God for taking our parents away and my dreams along with them. One night I dreamed they were alive and we were all happy again. They took me shopping and bought me nice clothing. I went to boarding school. It was a wonderful dream, and my disappointment was even heavier when I awoke and found it was just a fantasy. I cried real tears to God and asked, "Why did you let me dream such a nice dream and then wake up to this?" Sophie sucked in her breath and then bent over her straw to take in more soda. "Soon after we met Daddy Tom. I never believed my life could be this good. Here I am in a beautiful home. I attend boarding school." She raised her bottle. "I have all this and I can now afford to drink soda. Never have I had pocket money for soda! God has blessed me so much!" With her emotions spilling over, she clasped her hand over her mouth and fled the tiny room.

Robert, Rachel and I stared at our shoes, swallowing hard and clear-ing our throats. Rubbing my eyes, I looked over the humble home for which Sophie was so grateful. The cement walls had been painted bright green long ago and were now peeling and badly scuffed. Taped to the wall were a couple old posters announcing revivals in the area. Somehow they had pounded a nail into the wall and hung a family photo from my wife,

Sarah. An electric fan struggled to cool us as we silently waited. As the breeze gently rocked the curtain hanging across their open doorway, I spotted a basin of water with their lunch dishes soaking outside. Next to it was a pile of ashes where they had cooked a simple meal of soy beans. *If I lived here with these conditions, would I feel that same sense of gratitude? Would I be praising God and saying He has blessed me so much? Would I be saying, "I never believed my life could be this good?"*

My thoughts are interrupted with, "Daddy, I want milk." I open my eyes to see my little daughter standing next to my bed. I scoop her up and gently place her between Sarah and me. "Okay. You wait here. I'll get you some."

When I return she is asleep. I stroke her hair and watch her lying there so peaceful and secure. *She has no idea how blessed she is to live in this house with a mommy and daddy who love her and take care of her. She'll never know what it is to be hungry. She doesn't have to worry about collecting firewood. If she ever sleeps on the floor, it will be because she wants to and she'll have a sleeping bag and carpet beneath her.*

Wide awake now I decide to stay up and work in my office. As I walk past my bookcase a photo catches my eye. I stop to pick it up. Grace and her children. How could I ever forget them? I remember how sick she was and how she gave me a chicken and eggs when she could have used them so much more than I. I recall the fear in her son Godfrey's eyes when he urged me to come and pray for his mother.

Grace and Rachel became instant friends on Rachel's first trip to Uganda. She and Robert built a house for Grace. They wanted her children to attend boarding school so they can become doctors or teachers or whatever they desire to do instead of remaining stuck in the cycle of destitution. Grace readily agreed so they committed to paying the children's tuition for as long as the children want to attend. Whenever Grace sees Rachel approaching her house she runs to her with arms outstretched, crying joyfully and the two of them grab one another and dance around. Last time Rachel was in Uganda she told Grace: "Grace, you have inspired me to write about the women of Uganda. Although we are great friends I really know so little about you. Would you tell me your story?"

Abandoned by her mother when she was two years old, Grace was raised by one of her father's other wives. After that wife died, Grace was shifted around to different family members including uncles who sexually abused her. She married at a young age hoping to escape her life of oppression. Unable to bear children, she was convinced a demon lived in the house preventing her from having babies. She moved from one relationship to another hoping to overcome this problem. Beatings by boyfriends were common and she accepted them as a way of life until one day the man she lived with thrashed her badly, stripped her naked and threw her out of the house. Humiliated and scared Grace slunk from the house trying to hide her nudity. The man's mother saw her, took pity on her and gave her a dress. Grace returned to her father. "I've been beaten and sent away with nothing."

"You can't have a successful marriage because the habits of your mother have followed you."

Finally Grace became pregnant. Happy that the curse was broken, she wanted to return to the man who disgraced her. Friends were angered and admonished: "That man who beat you and removed your clothes and everyone saw your nakedness and you want to go back to him?"

She did not want to stay with the baby's father so she looked for and found her mother. She introduced herself and told her she had suffered her whole life. Her mother was sorry and asked her to stay. Grace delivered her baby and remained with her mother until another man came along. She lived with him for a number of years and had three children with him. Suddenly he turned against her and left, taking everything with him. "He didn't even leave a matchbook."

A survivor and a hard worker, Grace started buying and selling fish. She was able to save enough money to buy a plot of land and worked to buy another plot alongside the road and put up a shop. Her husband returned and was going back and forth between Grace and his new wife and one day sold one of her plots of land. Grace went to the authorities and he was put in jail, but immediately upon being released he took everything from Grace's shop and brought it to his other wife. Then he sold that plot too and took the children! He said: "Now let me see what you can do! I've taken the children and now I'm going to kill you!"

Eventually he returned the children as they were too much trouble and were extremely malnourished. Grace and her children moved to a one room rental. She was sick. Her husband had infected her with AIDS. One Saturday she woke up and started thinking about all he had done to her and how he had taken away everything she had worked for, and now she would die because of him. As her rage boiled, she decided to kill him and cooked a meal for him mixed with poison. She heard a voice: "Why do you want to kill this man? The land the man robbed you of you got by working the soil with your hands. You can work again and restore what was taken." She threw the food away and the next day went to church and accepted Christ.

God has given back much more than was ever taken. She is in a program and receives antiretroviral drugs and most of the time feels pretty good. She is happy that her children are being educated. She loves her new home and has goats and a cow and chickens. She loves the Lord and wants to serve Him.

Last time we were in Uganda, a team built a new mud kitchen for Grace. It is huge! Along with her new kitchen, she received new pots and pans and a charcoal roaster! She thinks life is good.

Placing the photo back on the shelf I pray things will be different for this new generation of women coming up. I have heard far too many tales of women being exploited, beaten and treated as animals. Women say the reason they are treated like property is because the husband pays a dowry, and he thinks that means he owns his wife like he owns his cattle.

I sit at my desk and consider the lives of the Ugandans. Life has not been easy for them. Thirty years after Idi Amin's reign of terror, people are still talking about it and recalling the atrocities. They say he was so merciless he killed his own son and removed his heart. Each soldier was given a weapon and told: "That is your pay. Your gun is your parent. If you want to eat or if you need anything, use your weapon to get it." No one was safe whether they lived in town or in the bush. The soldiers were everywhere. People remember the fear of going to bed at night and wondering if they would be dragged from their beds to be raped, killed or tortured by the soldiers. During the day they wondered if they would be alive to go to bed at night. One never knew what bush a soldier would be hiding behind. It was a senseless, brutal time. They showed me the river where the soldiers took people piled in the back of a dump truck; backed up to the river and dumped them alive. They were unable to swim and those who tried were shot from the shore. Some say 300,000 died at the hand of Amin and his soldiers. Others say as many as 500,000 were killed. Today there is the Lord's Resistance Army. Rachel and Robert traveled to the Soroti refugee camps. As they strolled through the camps, they heard accounts of people fleeing the rebels. A woman of fifty told how the rebels attacked and beat her so badly her legs were now useless. She said: "I almost died. Family members carried me to a vehicle and sent me here to this camp. Before the rebels came, life was peaceful and we had plenty to eat. Now I have lived here for three years. I will never walk again. I don't know when I can go home or if I will have a home to go to."

Sixty-year-old Regina talked of her life prior to the rebels. "Our children were growing up in a good atmosphere. They were well-fed with clean noses and clean eyes. Women could do any kind of work including building houses." One day Regina was at the well when Ugandan soldiers approached and asked her if she knew where the rebels were. Suddenly rebels rushed from nowhere and killed all the Ugandan soldiers. Regina fell to the ground and remained still until she was sure the rebels were gone. She stood and immediately walked the twenty-five miles to Soroti with only the clothes on her back. It has been three years since Regina fled her comfortable home, and now she sleeps on grass she gathers around the camp. Her brother's children have all been abducted and have not been heard of since.

Isaac said he was at the well when the rebels ambushed him, removed all his clothes and took him to the bush for three weeks. Usually new captives are immediately forced to witness or take part in killings. Some are ordered to steal or destroy property and to abuse dead bodies while others are made to kill a family member or friend. Some actually go mad from the horror of it all while others turn into monsters like their captors. Isaac said most just want to go home. He was one of the lucky ones and managed to escape, but the mass destruction he experienced and witnessed will remain with him for all his life.

How do you comfort such people? There are no words. Again we ask: "Where are you, God? Do you see what is happening to these people? Do you care?"

I stand to look out my office window. Darkness is fading. Soon my family will be rising. It is Sunday and we will dress up for church. In Uganda if you own shoes, you wear them to church and dress in your best clothes. If you don't have shoes and your clothes have holes in them, you go anyway. No one cares. They are happy to have you there. Church is a joyful meeting as people dance and sing and laugh and talk and pray. They don't know about getting ahead in this world and the drive to own expensive cars, big houses with swimming pools and wearing the latest fashion. They know about loving one another and helping their brothers and sisters and serving the Lord with all their hearts. They care for their sisters who are dying. They hold hands, hug and share whatever they have. They value one another and hurt when their neighbors hurt. They rejoice when good things happen to their friends.

I hear my coffee pot starting and decide to go over some more papers while I waited for my coffee. I took out the plans for the new hospital… Our clinic was successful in saving lives, but after seeing what patients are subjected to in the public hospitals, I knew we had to do more. We began planning for a state-or-the-art hospital. We visualized modern, sterile equipment; clean beds with mattress covers so the mattresses wouldn't smell of urine. We dreamed of a friendly atmosphere with high quality and compassionate staff who treat patients because it is their job.

Back in the States I began sharing this vision. An eighteen-year-old girl in California was deeply touched and told her parents: "I want to give my $100,000 trust fund to Hope4Kids so they can build a hospital." Two churches in California, Messiah Lutheran in Los Angeles and the Lutheran Church of the Good Shepherd in Torrance, aggressively raised funds.

Last November we dedicated the new hospital. Dr. Stephen Malinga, minister of health from the Ugandan president's office, was the guest of honor. Among the attendees that day were parliament members and city officials as well as pastors from the area and Kenya and Tanzania. The VIPs toured the grounds and Pastor Wilber and I gave an account of each building's use and our plans for the future. With great ceremony the foundation stone was unveiled and the tour through the hospital began. Dr. Stephen was impressed with our plan for a preemie ward. He asked, "Are you sure you want that? It's very expensive to have a heart monitor, oxygen, incubators and all you need." He paused. "But then, there isn't a preemie ward in all of Eastern Uganda.…"

In his speech to the crowd, Dr. Stephen praised our efforts and thanked us for following the footsteps of Jesus by caring for the widows and orphans. He talked about the tremendous need for prenatal care and urged men to attend classes with their wives. "Don't leave the responsibility of pregnancy and childbearing to women. Every woman should have prenatal care and should deliver in a hospital or health care center." He said when he visited Chicago's Southside, some time ago, they were very upset with the rate of twelve babies out of 1000 dying before they reach the age of one year. In Uganda the death rate in the first year of life is 100 out of 1000. He said in Chicago's Southside mothers dying in childbirth was very high according to American standards. At that time eleven mothers out of 100,000 died in childbirth. In Uganda there are 506 mothers per 100,000 dying in childbirth each year. "We lose a lot of mothers unnecessarily because they hemorrhage and die at home. If they were in the hospital this could easily be prevented."

Dr. Stephen also stated, "Abstinence for young people is the position of the government. And if you are married, *please* stick to one partner! I am obliged to tell you that if you cannot help yourself, use a condom, but what I want to tell you is abstain and stick to one partner."

I set down my papers and sneak to the kitchen. If I could just have one cup of coffee before the kids get up… As I inhale the aroma and pour myself a cup, I remember the triplets who were born while we were in Uganda. The whole village talked about this miracle! They were born in a mud hut at four in the morning! Their father delivered them by the dim light of a candle. Rachel saw them when they were just hours old. She was immediately drawn to the third born, a girl, and said, "That's my baby!" Several months later when she returned and checked on the babies, they were sick, and she along with team members loaded the triplets into a van and took them to our hospital. When their mother, Jane, registered them, she said the little girl's name was Rachel. She turned to Rachel and said, "You said, 'that's my baby' so I named her after you."

Rachel held baby Rachel and prayed over her and talked to her. Delighted when the baby cooed and tried to talk, Rachel fell totally in love with her baby. When baby Rachel was seven months old, Rachel went to see her, bringing clothes and gifts for all three babies and found Baby Rachel to be very tiny. She asked Jane, "Is she sick?"

"No. She's okay. She's just hungry. We are out of the baby formula you bought last time."

Rachel and her friends rushed to town to buy more formula and brought it right away. They also gave the babies sippy cups because the doctor said the mother did not sterilize the bottles properly, so he suggested they use cups.

Two days later Rachel was told Baby Rachel died. They had already buried her by the time Rachel arrived at their home. Jane came running out and said, "Rachel. Your baby is gone." Pointing to a mound of dirt with a cross made of two sticks tied together, she added, "She's there."

Rachel knelt next to the tiny grave and cried. Her heart broke for the mother who had told her: "Before you came to help me, I thought about running away and leaving my eleven children. But you gave me hope." Looking up at Jane, Rachel thought she looked way too tired for a thirty-two-year-old woman. She fingered the crude little cross and thought about all the little Rachels who would never make it to their first birthday. She stood and held Jane tightly, praying there would be an end to the poverty and heartache in this home. She wondered about Jane's future and what it must be like to have to share her husband with his other family who lived in Kenya. She wondered how many nights Jane felt alone.... I pick up my newspaper and settle down with my coffee to read. There are a heap of ads for Christmas. There are articles on dealing with the stress of the holidays. Stress of the holidays? What is stress? People are stressing about seeing family members they don't particularly like and what kinds of gifts should be showered upon their kids. How *will they pay for it all? Oh. And will I get my Christmas cards out on time? Okay. Let's put this in perspective. What is stress really? Does a little kid in Uganda know what stress is when he loses his parents to AIDS and wonders where his next meal is coming from and where he will live and how he will survive and will he die too? Now that's stress!*

I toss the ads aside and kneel in prayer. *God, help me to keep this all in perspective. As we see the needs around us this Christmas and throughout the year help us to make a difference and to understand what You require of us.*

Chapter Four

What is Required of You?

tanding alone, stripped to my boxer shorts, I shivered in the cold, bare room. I was arrested at the border trying to cross into the then Soviet Union carrying Bibles and Christian literature. I waited to see what my destiny would be.

I had smuggled Bibles into the Soviet Union a number of times and had close calls, but God always seemed to shut the eyes of the border patrol, and each time I had been successful in getting Bibles into the hands of believers. The first time I crossed the border in 1973, my van was left in shambles by the guards. They even ripped out the lining of the ceiling, yet failed to find the Bibles I had hidden in my clothing. Why was I caught this time?

Another time I flew into the Soviet Union with a tour group. As we boarded the Russian airliner in Amsterdam, the hand of the guard who frisked me hit a Bible. Instinctively I twisted just as his hand returned to the same place...to find my wallet.

In line at the customs desk in Leningrad, the two women in front of me were asked if they had any books or magazines. I rummaged through my mind, wondering how to honestly answer that question when the customs official asked, "Do you have any fruits or vegetables?"

"No."

I had witnessed miraculous border crossings. Why was I arrested now? Had I become overconfident in my own abilities? Had I done something not pleasing to our Lord? Would I have been safe if I had more faith? Would I ever see my family again? What would happen to me? What would happen to my associate, Joe, who was being interrogated in another room?

Three surly guards strode into the room, banging the massive, metal door shut behind them. I was scrutinized with a vengeance. Their fury seemed to become more severe with each question they fired at me.

"What are you intending to do here? Why have you come? Why did you bring these illegal books?" Three sets of icy, uncompromising eyes glared waiting for answers.

"Is it wrong to bring Bibles?"

"Yes! It is wrong to bring Bibles and you are under arrest!"

I swallowed hard, trying not to stare at their clenched fists and massive, coarse knuckles. The pitch in my voice raised a few octaves. "But I read in *Soviet Life* magazine and other publications that there is freedom of religion here. So your magazines must tell lies."

"No!" A fist slammed down on the metal table top. "You do not understand. We do have freedom, but Bibles are illegal."

"But Soviet pastors have lectured in America and…"

"We even take Bibles from pastors!"

My palms were damp with sweat and my voice sounded like I was going through my second adolescence. "So it is illegal to have Bibles?"

"Yes!"

"Is this a new law?"

"No. It is an old law."

"Then why have Soviet tour guides told us that Bibles are plentiful and there is no religious persecution?"

"No Bibles! Bibles are illegal!" Another fist struck the table.

Since I had not slept on the long flight from Seattle to Amsterdam to

Leningrad; I had been awake for about thirty-six hours. I fought exhaustion as the interrogation wore on. I struggled to bring Scripture to mind.

"Whenever you are arrested and brought to trial, do not worry beforehand about what to say. Just say whatever is given you at the time, for it is not you speaking, but the Holy Spirit" (Mark 13:11). Recalling God's promises brought a sense of peace, boldness and awareness that I was in my Heavenly Father's hands. The guards could do nothing to me unless my Father allowed it.

Brother Andrew, author of *God's Smuggler,* (2006)[5] smuggled Bibles to Idi Amin's soldiers during the height of Amin's reign of terror. Later he was interviewed on national television where the host questioned the danger involved in such activities. Brother Andrew responded: "Danger? What is danger? There is only one danger. That is to be out of the will of God. If it is the will of God that I be in Idi Amin's army distributing Bibles, I am as safe there as if I stayed home."

With renewed confidence, I told my captors I brought Bibles because it was the most important book in my life. Trusting in the author of the Bible had changed my life from one of hatred to love. I had come to the Soviet Union to deliver the Bread of Life to anyone who would take it because I loved the Russian people. I looked into the unyielding eyes of each of the three Soviet men and said, "I love you too."

The grilling continued. In the midst of their wrath and loathing, I sensed a tranquility that could only come from God. My voice was strong. "Yes. I believe. I believe the Bible is the most special book ever written, and I believe what it teaches. My desire is to share the Good News of this book with the Russian people."

Finally, after hours of interrogation, I was asked to sign a paper admitting my guilt to smuggling illegal contraband. When I checked my suitcases, I saw they had confiscated all my Russian Bibles and literature as well as some of my clothing and money. When I questioned the guards, one asked, "Do you want to make additional trouble?"

I shook my head.

Joe and I were escorted to the back seat of a waiting car. Uncertain of what would happen next, we did not speak on the ride into Leningrad. The driver pulled up to a hotel and dropped us off.

As we unpacked we talked through what had just happened to us. We agreed we had been a part of a battle that was bigger than the KGB (Russian police). I had sensed an evil about the guards and could almost hear the swords of the spiritual warriors clash as I was under attack. Since the guards had no personal reason to be angry about the Bibles, I believe they were driven by an unseen force. Satan hates the Scripture. The Bible says he is deceptive and takes on many disguises to accomplish his mission to destroy the work of Christ. He comes as a roaring lion, a subtle angel of light or as a menacing Soviet guard. "For our struggle is not against flesh and blood, but against the rulers, against the authorities, against the powers of this dark world and against the spiritual forces of evil in the heavenly realms" (Ephesians 6:12).

Christians are equipped for battle with Satan and his army. The sixth chapter of Ephesians goes on to tell us that God gives us: the belt of truth, the breastplate of God's approval, shoes that are able to speed us on to carry God's good news, the shield of faith to protect us from the darts the evil forces throw at us, the helmet of salvation, and the sword of the Spirit, which is God's Word.

Just over a week after our arrest at the border, Joe and I were hitchhiking and a university professor picked us up. We asked him if we could speak to one of his classes. He thought that would be impossible as our countries were experiencing strained relations at the time. The Americans had just boycotted the Olympics in response to the Soviet invasion of Afghanistan. The professor thought about it a little longer then agreed he would like us to attend his class but cautioned us to be careful. We attempted to dress like the students so we wouldn't stand out.

We expected only to observe the class so were surprised when we were introduced as the guest speakers. Joe started out by talking about Russian history and eventually the subject of God came up. The students laughed.

"God's just a fairy tale," one scoffed.

"Only the simple believe in God," another offered.

"The Bible is just a fairy tale book."

"If the Bible is just a fairy tale book," I countered, "then why were we arrested at your border ten days ago for bringing Bibles into your country? I challenge you. The government is hiding something from you. If these are worthless books, why would they go to all the effort of keeping them from you? That book has stood the test of time, and I challenge you to try to get a hold of a copy and read what's in there."

The mood of the classroom changed from mockery to curiosity and they asked question after question. The professor invited us to attend his afternoon class, but after lunch he told us that all the conversations in the cafeteria had been about our visit to his class, and now the KGB were looking for us. We were disappointed to have to leave, but the message of God's love was spreading through the university.

I first began smuggling Bibles into the Communist Soviet Union in 1973. Because of the anti-American sentiment, my partner, Brad, and I did not want to be recognized as Americans and attempted to dress European. We attended the Baptist church in Moscow. At that time, according to Soviet constitution, religion was legal. A few churches remained open to silence the critics from the free world. These churches were closely monitored by the KGB. Pastors would be arrested if they preached the true gospel.

Outside the church we were approached by a teenage girl. Without looking at us, she said, "I must speak to you but not here. Meet me down two blocks and to the left." Quickly she slipped away. Walking hastily to the spot, we found her sitting on a park bench with an older man. She promptly introduced herself as Natasha and her father, Vladimir.

We had been trained to ask certain questions when we met up with people claiming to be Believers to make sure we weren't being trapped by the KGB. Vladimir realized what we were doing and with eyes twinkling said, "We're really the KGB."

Natasha instructed us to follow them at a distance and they led us to their apartment. Quickly she ushered us inside and pulled the window shades. Within the confines of their sparsely furnished apartment, they spoke in hushed voices. Natasha stated simply, "You have brought us bread".

"Yes. How did you know?"

"We were praying and God told us two Americans were coming, and they would bring us Bibles. I was not sure when I saw you. I thought maybe you were from the Ukraine, but my spirit felt your spirit and I knew you were the ones."

We spent the next couple of hours hearing their story. Natasha's father had been a student of Marxism at the University of Moscow. He had written award winning papers on Marx, the founder of communism and also on Lenin, the Soviet revolutionaryleader. His research led him to a propaganda magazine strongly criticizing Christians for their faith. He began to wonder about these Christians. He wondered if they actually had something worth believing in. Being the curious scholar, he studied the life of Christ which led him to believe in Jesus as the Son of God. He put his trust in Him and courageously began to live for Him.

Arrested for sharing his faith, the government snatched his wife and young son from their home. Vladimir did not know where they had taken his wife, but he knew his son would be taken to a child care institution where he would be trained in communism. One day the authorities called Vladimir and told him to come and pick up his son. He and Natasha joyfully rushed to the designated place. Government officials stood on the steps holding the boy firmly between them. Oh the delight when Natasha and Vladimir saw him! The officials stopped them a few feet from the boy. "Deny Christ and the boy can go home. Refuse and you will not see him again." With a breaking heart, Vladimir knew he could never deny his Lord. The boy was taken away and no more contact was allowed.

Their apartment was set on fire, and when Vladimir walked down the street, people threw rocks at him. He was beaten by the police and constantly harassed.

Natasha was thirteen and refused to join the young communist party. When her classmates wore their uniforms to school, the teacher asked

Natasha why she did not wear hers. "I am not going to join the young pioneers, because I believe in God. I love Jesus and I am not ashamed to say so." As soon as she spoke the name of Jesus, her teacher began slapping her face and told her to never speak that name again. Other teachers slapped her and beat her. Classmates were encouraged to laugh and make fun of her for believing in Jesus.

Natasha told us: "When they beat me, I pray that they will see the love of Jesus in me so they too can meet Him and have eternal life…they have taken away my mama. They have taken away my brother. All they have left to do is to take away my papa. But they will never take away my Jesus."

Too soon it was time for us to leave and we brought out the Bibles. They explained that Bibles were in such short supply that these Bibles would be torn apart and shared with other Christians. Each page was precious and would be cherished. Natasha and Vladimir wanted to pray for us before we left. I could not hold back tears as they lay prostrate on the floor and poured their hearts out to the Lord. I listened as Natasha prayed for their enemies and prayed for us. She had only love in her voice. No whining or asking God why they had to go through all this persecution. Only "Thank you, Jesus, for our difficulties because they make us strong."

We were able to meet Natasha and Vladimir in the forest the next day. Again I was struck by how their focus was not upon themselves or their problems. Their passion was to serve Jesus and then others in whatever capacity they felt called. I brought a tape recorder and taped messages from them to Christians in America. Over and over I have listened to Natasha's voice as she greeted: "My dear brothers and sisters in America. I am very happy that I have possible to say for you something. My best wish for you with all my heart; I want so that you would become a witness of God everywhere, for every person to say about Jesus. So everyone who does not know Jesus can come to Him, to know Him. And you be a light of God where you live.…"

I kept in touch with Natasha and Vladimir over the next years. They remained forever faithful to God and were constantly persecuted and mocked for believing in Jesus. "Consider it pure joy, my brothers, whenever you face trials of many kinds, because you know that the testing of your faith develops perseverance" (James 1:2-3).

Vladimir did not live to see the fall of communism, and Natasha was able to immigrate to France just before the communist government collapsed in August of 1991. I have since lost track of her, but I believe she is somewhere in this world serving our Lord in a freedom which she could never have dreamed.

In August of 1991, I was headed to Moscow to speak at the Moscow Gospel Music Festival. Two days after the tanks surrounded the Federation Building where Yeltsin was holed up, I was staying in a hotel close enough to watch the human barricades standing before the military tanks. I took pictures out my window of the young people standing for freedom.

One day after the coup ended we opened the music festival. We were giving away one million New Testaments. We had to have guards protecting our Bibles because people were trampling one another for a copy.

One evening after the Holy Smoke band from Denver gave a concert, I delivered a message. I was shaking as I began. Yeltsin's parliament men had come in, showed their badges, and kicked people out of the front rows in order to sit there. After eighteen years of being followed by the KGB and having to secretly tell people about Christ, I can not begin to express the pleasure I felt at openly declaring to these newly freed Russians of the further freedom they could experience by living for Jesus. I asked those who wanted to know that liberty and desired to accept Christ as Savior to stand. My tears flowed freely as most of the audience rose to their feet. I became so emotional I could not pray. Someone had to take over for me while I stood in the wings weeping. A navy officer approached. *Maybe I shouldn't have told that part about being arrested at the border.*

"Young man, I just wanted to come and thank you. I have given my heart to God tonight. I want to know if I can give you a hug."

Sveta, my translator, had angrily told me she did not like what I was doing, and we had no business bringing our Christianity to Moscow. She was one of the many who accepted Christ that night. A few years later when my friends from Montana, David and Susan, adopted Katya, Sveta lived with them as Katya's translator.

One elderly man asked if it was true God forgives every wrong we have committed. When I assured him it was, he said, "I want to believe you, but it is so difficult after having been told for the past seventy years that there is no God."

A few days later the Holy Smoke Band performed at Yeltsin's victory party and presented him with our one millionth Bible.

In Leningrad I spoke from the steps of the museum of atheism. An elderly woman knelt on a piece of cardboard and cried, "I always thought the Americans would come with weapons of war, but, instead they are bringing the gospel of peace." A team member presented her with a Bible and asked if she had ever owned one. She answered: "I have been a Christian all my life. I lost my husband and two children during World War II. Every day God has given me the strength through eleven scraps of paper of His Word. Every morning I line them up on my breakfast table and read them. Today is the first day I have had my own Bible."

In the summer of 2003 I led a team to Russia. This was my fifty-third trip there in thirty years. One night a few of us walked to a hotel in downtown St. Petersburg for a cup of coffee. On our way back to the metro, we realized we were going the wrong way, so we turned back. A team member showed me a map and I recognized a name in the upper corner. "Myla, I know this guy! Where did you get this map?"

"He was standing on the corner and asked if we needed a guide, and I told him no, but he handed me the map and said I could have it for a souvenir."

"We've got to find him!" We ran in the direction of the street corner, and here in a city of five million I was reunited with my friend, Sasha. I had not seen him since 1988.

I met Sasha in 1986 when I was still smuggling Bibles into the Soviet Union. Mark Hedman and I were standing on a sidewalk and Sasha came up. "Oh my God! Americans!" Not many Americans traveled to Russia in those days.

I asked how he knew we were Americans. He looked down at my square toed boot and responded. "Your shoes. I can tell by your expensive shoes."

He offered to show us the city and took us to an underground coffee shop where intellectuals and musicians hung out. The shop was nick-named Saigon. There was a huge mirror along one wall. Later I found out this place was constantly under surveillance by the KGB and they sat behind this mirror watching what was going on.

In those days the government did not allow Western music or any music not approved by the government, so concerts were held in secret. They did however allow one rock band, Electrical Moving Force. Sasha of course knew the group, so he took Mark and me to one of their concerts and seated us in the front row. The police were watching every move of the crowd, and when some kids stood to dance they were told to sit down or the concert would be shut down. After a while they stood to dance again and the KGB stopped the concert. Sasha took us on stage to meet the band, and we gave them tapes of the group, Stryper, a popular Christian rock band. We had to run out of there because the KGB was chasing everyone, so we walked a ways and stood under a street lamp talk-ing with the band. Suddenly all of the street lights were turned off and we knew we had better move on.

Mark and I tried sharing Christ with Sasha who was an atheist. He was not interested but said he knew a Christian. A Baptist. Would we like to meet the Baptist? We met Dimitri at the Saigon, but he said it was not safe to talk there, so he would meet us at the Russian museum the following day. It would be easier to talk there without arousing suspicion. As we walked through the museum, Dimitri told us he had been so low he had decided to commit suicide. He received a letter from a Christian friend out-lining how to receive Christ and through this letter accepted Jesus as Savior. His parents were both nuclear scientists and had no need for such nonsense. Those beliefs were for old people and children. They turned him in to the secret police. He was committed to a mental hospital where shock treatment and mind-altering drugs were not successful in chasing away his faith. His father told him as far as he was concerned, Dimitri was dead.

Dimitri led others to Christ and would bring them to the Russian museum to show them a painting of Nero throwing the Christians to the lions. He encouraged young Christians facing persecution and harassment. "At least they are not throwing us to the lions. God will not allow us to suffer more than He can give us strength to bear." So, here I was reunited with Sasha after seventeen years. Whenever I had asked around about him, I was told he was in prison. During one of his prison terms he asked Jesus to be Lord of his life. He asked us to walk with him to his apartment. Books were stacked along the walls. He was documenting the history of Russia. Someone pointed to an autographed picture of Gorbachev and asked, "Is that authentic?"

"Yes. I've witnessed to him. He gave that to me." Then he took the picture off the wall and presented it to me. "Take it. I'll get another next time I see him."

Sasha told us about some of the times he had been arrested. He is an intellectual who protested the communist government. The Soviets had a newspaper called the Pravda, meaning Truth. Sasha printed an anti-Soviet Pravda paper and stood on street corners handing them out. He was repeatedly thrown in jail for his anti-Soviet activities.

Sasha's first arrest was in a demonstration against the war in Afghanistan. He was carrying a poster which translates to "Let's return our guys from Afghanistan while they are still alive." He was jailed fifteen days for taking part in public activity against the government.

In 1990, one year before the fall of communism, Sasha attended a session of parliament in Lenningrad which was broadcast live on TV. He sewed by hand a large Russian Flag of the days before communism. He stood on a balcony, and with the cameras rolling he unfurled his flag. The cameras froze on the flag and the session stopped. No one knew what to do. The democratic deputies blocked the assistant to the mayor from getting to Sasha. He was whispering threats and told him to throw down the flag or he would cut the belt off his pants forcing Sasha to drop the flag in order to preserve his dignity.

Sasha and his friends stayed up all night making minature Russian flags to hand out to deputies the next day. Parliament closed the palace in Lennigrad for two days and the mayor wanted to sue Sasha, but the TV station refused to support the law suit because it caused their ratings to go up. Sasha became sort of a folk hero after that.

Sasha proclaimed he loves his country and only wants to see true democracy and freedom for the Russian people.

As we were ready to leave, Sasha turned to Myla. "My mother is in the next room. She has just lost her husband and now she is dying of breast cancer. Will you come and pray for her?" Sasha motioned for me to join them. As we knelt next to his mother's bed, I marveled at our meeting and how here I was kneeling in prayer with a man who had been a strong atheist who was now asking God to perform a miracle of healing for his mother.

A few months after the fall of Nicolae Ceausescu, the feared Romanian Communist dictator, I was a keynote speaker at a youth conference in Oradea, Romania. Yuri, our host, said the day Ceausescu fell from power an announcement came over the radio saying there was an emergency, and everyone was ordered to remain in their homes. For several anxious hours, they waited next to the radio as music played continuously. Finally it was announced that Ceausescu had fled. Yuri felt the urgency to be with others, so he took a train to the center of the city. Already, seventy thousand people had gathered in front of the communist headquarters. A broadcast came over the loudspeakers declaring the dictator had been overthrown.

People cheered and danced with joy, crying and hugging one another. "Then," Yuri said, "everyone dropped to their knees and began reciting the Lord's Prayer and ended by saying, 'Our God is great!'"

Romanians were now free to worship God. "You, my brothers, were called to be free. But do not use your freedom to indulge the sinful nature;

rather, serve one another in love" (Galatians 5:13). While countries like Russia and Romania have been set free to worship, there are still places in the world like China where it is against the law to be a Christian. During the early 1980s there had been a great purge in China. Two hundred thousand people were arrested and according to some reports, thirty thousand were executed. It was not a good time to bring Bibles into China.

The borders were sealed, and no literature was being allowed in. Those who tried to bring in Bibles were stopped, arrested, and even executed. Yet I found myself leading a team of fifteen whose desire was to cross the border with Chinese Bibles.

Our sponsoring organization told us it had been difficult for anyone attempting to take literature into China and said they would rather we did not undertake such a momentous challenge at this time, but our team agreed we had come too far to turn back. And we agreed if we were going to be arrested for taking a little literature into the country, we would just as soon be arrested for taking a lot. We took all the material they would give us.

"If you make it," we were told, "this will be the largest shipment of Scriptures ever brought in by a group of couriers. Pray that you get the red star on your luggage tickets, which means you are okay and you probably won't be checked again."

When our train arrived at the Chinese border, the Hong Kong personnel got off the train, and the People's Republic of China representatives boarded. They asked for our passports and visas, checking to be sure they were in order. They also checked luggage, asking which bag belonged to whom. I prayed to get a red star on my declaration form and baggage tickets.

None of us received the red star, and as the train pulled away from the Hong Kong border, my throat was dry and my hands shook. What would happen when we arrived at the customs office in Canton? On that long, two-hour ride I stared out the window, watching the Chinese countryside streak by. I reflected upon a sermon I had preached about Joshua just a few days earlier.

Joshua was a brave man who was given the charge of bringing God's people into the land God had promised; yet they had a problem. There were already people living there who were much better equipped for battle.

The city of Jericho was the key to the conquest of the Promised Land. There was a great wall around the city, with houses and watchtowers built into it, and chariots driving all around it.

The guards in the watchtowers saw a strange sight. Joshua followed the Lord's command for taking the city and told seven priests to circle the wall once a day for seven days while blowing horns. Some armed men walked silently before the priests. The priests were followed by the ark of the Lord, which was symbolic of God's presence with the Israelites. The ark was followed by a rear guard.

The procession must have looked pretty harmless to the men in the watchtowers. Imagine what they must have reported to their superiors, "They're just walking around with their religious artifacts, blowing horns."

But Joshua and the people continued to follow the Lord's instruction. On the seventh day, they let out a trumpet blast and a shout, and the walls tumbled. Jericho belonged to God's people.

Like Joshua I had to rely on God to give me the strength and to trust the Lord beyond my own ability.

I prayed once more as the train slowly pulled into the station and we all grabbed our bags. In tense silence we made our way to the customs hall. Nervously I glanced around to see what was happening. I was the first in our group to take my place in the customs line. It seemed some were being let through without having their luggage searched. Still others had their suitcases opened by guards and the contents were scrutinized. Finally, it was my turn. I looked the young Chinese official squarely in the eyes, praying for the courage of Joshua while I answered a couple of routine questions. Within minutes he nodded for me to pass through. He hadn't asked me to open my suitcase. I wanted to shout! It was as though the walls of Jericho had crumbled. I stood silently by the city exit waiting for the rest of my group. All but one of us made it through without having to open our suitcases. The last person in our group was being questioned more thoroughly and they were digging through his carry-on. Fourteen of us held our breath. What would happen to our friend? Would we be separated? What would we do if he was sent back? Would they check all of us when they found his Bibles? We heard the official questioning him about books.

He simply opened his bag to show the officials two books about China he had purchased in Hong Kong. Finally they allowed him to pass through customs. We had safely brought in a precious shipment of Bibles for our Chinese brothers and sisters in Christ. Our prayer was answered and now we had to cautiously deliver the Scriptures to our contacts so they could be given to those believers who did not have Bibles.

Like a good spy novel, we met and exchanged bags with people who were dressed like Hong Kong and Chinese peasants. Eventually word got back to us that the mission was accomplished.

Sun, our Chinese national guide, was an intelligent twenty-five-year-old man who spoke five languages fluently, and he used every one of them to tell us he was an atheist. He claimed he believed only in himself; but one night, he found his way to my hotel room. He was facing some difficult struggles. He said he didn't want to live another day, and the odds were if he didn't find some answers, he wouldn't. He spilled out the pain of his loneliness and despair for an hour and a half.

I told him I could identify with his feelings of suicide because I had experienced them many times in my teen years. I shared how Jesus Christ had brought meaning and purpose to my life. He listened attentively as I told him about the life of Jesus and the promise of life with a purpose when committed to living for Christ. He gladly received the Chinese New Testament and literature on how to become a Christian. Late that evening, he left my room promising to read the books and disappeared for about thirty-six hours. When he finally showed up at the hotel restaurant, he said he had read the entire Bible and all the literature. "What is the ritual to become a Christian?"

"There's no ritual. You simply pray, ask God for forgiveness of your sins, and surrender your life to Jesus Christ."

He immediately did so.

Over the next two weeks, Sun carried his New Testament wherever we went, and at the conclusion of our tour he said: "Before you came, my heart thought about suicide. Now it thinks about Jesus. It was God's will that you came."

Four years later I received word that Sun was attending a university in Vancouver, British Columbia. He was growing in his Christian walk. He had not dared attend church in China for fear of losing his job and the opportunity to study in Canada, but he read his Bible daily and prayed without ceasing.

"Some days I would sense Jesus standing with me," he said.

In his book, *Wild at Heart,* John Eldridge claims:

> A man must have a battle to fight, a great mission to his life that involves and yet transcends even home and family. He must have a cause to which he is devoted even unto death, for this is written into the fabric of his being.[6]

Seventeen-year-old Hector was a Bible Student in Havana, Cuba and found such a cause when Castro came to power in 1961. When Hector's family prepared to flee Cuba, he refused to go. Even though his mother sobbed and pleaded, Hector believed God would have him remain. Tearfully she warned him he would severely suffer under Castro. He told her: "My purpose is to serve God and the people of Cuba here. He will give me strength. He is faithful."

When I met Pastor Hector in 2002 he had served two separate prison terms. They are not nice to you in Cuban prisons. Tortured for his faith, today he still proclaims, "God is faithful!" While his every move is under the government's scrutiny, he is allowed to oversee 500 churches in all of

Cuba. Since the Pope's visit in the late 1980s Cubans have experienced a new, but limited freedom of religion. In our journeys there, we have met many followers of Jesus who have groaned in agony at the hands of an intolerant government. Every Cuban pastor we encountered had spent time in jail.

We were assigned Communist security men as guides when we took teams into Cuba. There are armed guards everywhere. Whenever we called for a cab, a guard would stop the driver and ask where he was taking us. At our hotel our conversations were listened to and we had reason to believe our rooms and phones were bugged. We didn't feel threatened by any of this. We had nothing to hide and had permission from our government to travel to Cuba.

On our second trip they sent a guide who had a high position in government to watch our moves. We called him the General. When he introduced himself to the group, he appeared hostile and gave a speech about how great communism is and bragged about the goodness of Castro. "The people are well taken care of and don't need any of what you are bringing. I know you are here to undermine our system by promoting your own politics. Your former President Clinton said if the embargo couldn't overthrow Castro's government, maybe our friendship would."

Pat, our chairman of the board assured, the general we had not been told that and "Besides, Tom doesn't know anything about politics!" We cared about kids, and kids do not care about politics. We brought medicine and gifts for kids in hospitals and were there to simply share out of our abundance to children in need.

I was not surprised by the general's speech. I had heard it before. The first time I brought medicine to a hospital in Havana, I was told the hospital did not need our medicine. The government provided everything and they were well taken care of.

"That's great," I replied. "Here is a list of the medicine we have brought. Would you like to take a look at it?"

I handed it to the doctor and she gasped when she read it. Her hand shook a little and tears threatened to spill over when she looked up at me and said quietly, "Maybe we could use these things."

Under the watchful eye of the general we helped with the construction of the first new church building permitted in forty-two years! The pastor told us it had taken over seven years to obtain the building permit. They had been meeting in an open air makeshift church with an awning made from scraps of tin above the platform and the first eight rows. If it rained the people huddled under the tin cover. The police and government officials in the area acknowledged the church was changing the neighborhood and admitted crime had dropped significantly. Lives were being transformed!

We found a similar story when we traveled to the other side of the island to a fishing village near Cienfuego. This neighborhood had gotten so dangerous the police stayed away. Whenever they entered the area gangs attacked them and overturned their vehicles. A young, brave pastor and his wife decided to start a church in the middle of the neighborhood. Many criminals were changed by the power of Christ and had been called out of the darkness to the Light. The police approached the young pastor and told him, "We don't know what you are doing but keep it up." We walked safely through the village talking and laughing with the locals who were overjoyed at the change.

"Have I not commanded? Be strong and courageous. Do not be terrified; do not be discouraged, for the Lord your God will be with you wherever you go!" (Joshua 1:9)

Our general was at our side everywhere we went. He watched us pass out gifts to the children in the hospital. He was there when the doctors were presented with our offerings of medicine. He walked with us through the radically changed neighborhoods. He even went to church. He watched our team lovingly reach out to those in need. He saw the Spanish/English Bibles we distributed.

When it was time to say goodbye he was emotional. He said; "I have never met anyone like you and your group. I have never seen anyone doing what you are doing. You really are here to serve the people of Cuba."

I gave him a Spanish/English New Testament. Each team member had written a personal note inside the cover thanking him for being our guide. He smiled widely. "I was going to ask you if I could have one." I had highlighted some scripture and pointed to 1 John 3:17 explaining, "This is why we do what we do." I showed him what my parents showed me years ago. "If anyone has material possessions and sees his brother in need but has no pity on him, how can the love of God be in him?"

The first time Rachel and Robert were in Cuba, they fell immediately in love with the country and the people. Havana. It was exactly as they seen it in the Buena Vista Social Club documentary. Buildings were old. Streets were narrow. Music played everywhere and the people were happy and friendly.

With armed military men everywhere, they felt no danger as we walked the streets. An elderly, toothless woman approached me begging for money. I pointed to Rachel and whispered, "She's got lots of money. Go ask her." She ran to Rachel laughing. Putting an arm around her Rachel pointed back to me. "He lies. He's the one with lots of money." She ran back to me. More teasing. More laughter. Then I gently slipped my hand into hers, pressing money into it. Normally we do not encourage beggars but every once in awhile someone catches your eye…then your heart… and you just can not help yourself.

One of the charms of Cuba is they are still driving cars from the 1950s and earlier! Whenever we were to take a cab we tried to get a vintage car. The police always stopped the driver to ask where he was taking us, and once we had their permission we could enjoy the ride. One night Robert and I and four other guys wanted to go in a 1937 convertible. The woman cab driver said it was illegal to take so many, but if one ducked down whenever we saw a policeman, she would take us. The night was filled with laughter with all of us crammed into the car and trying to duck down to dodge the police. We rode along the Malecon and howled when the waves dashed over the brick wall. One of the joys of living in a restricted country is the people get such a delight when they think they are getting by with something. Their humor is incredible.

Before we went to Cuba, Rachel bought a DVD of Buena Vista Social Club and watched it over and over. She fell in love with one of the singers, Compay Segundo, who at the filming was ninety years old. She wondered if he were still alive, and one day when she and Robert were hanging around an open book market, she spotted a book, *The Buena Vista Social Club*. Snatching it up she showed it to Robert who was engaged in a conversation with a security guard. The guard nodded his approval at the book and Rachel asked, "Is Compay Segundo still alive?"

"Yes. In fact he is perfo rming tonight at the Hotel Nacional."

Rachel could not believe it! A chance to see Compay? Bubbling with excitement, she found me and asked if I could get tickets. I did. What a thrill. They do not have laws about videotaping and taking photos at concerts, so we were able to walk up front and kneel at his feet taking photo after photo. Rachel would run up, kneel and take photos, then return to her seat and exclaim, "I just sat at the feet of Compay Segundo!" She declared she could have gone home that night and felt the entire trip was worth those moments, but we had more to do.

Rachel manages to make friends quickly and happily goes home with anyone who invites her. I do not recommend it but how do you control your sister? She found herself in the home of seventy-eight-year-old Lousia who had lived in the same humble home for fifty-five years. In Cuba you cannot move without permission and you have to have good reason for the government to approve your move. It can not be because you just got married and do not want to live with your parents. So even though Louisa did not own her home, she would live in it until she dies. Then her daughter and granddaughter who were currently living with her would in a sense inherit it.

The windows had no glass and there was no door on the house. Her little kitchen had a worn linoleum covered floor. Her little apartment sized refrigerator looked like something from 1950. The living room kind of flowed from the kitchen and Louisa invited Rachel and her friends to sit in the sparsely furnished room. A flimsy wire fence surrounded the yard with an equally flimsy gate that could be locked to discourage intruders.

Louisa spoke English very well. She remembered the Revolution and the way Cuba was before Castro came to power but like most Cubans said little about politics. Rachel asked if she had a Bible. She did. She said she used to have an English Bible but did not know what happened to it. Rachel took her Spanish Bible, turned to Isaiah 6:8 and told her, "Listen to this. This is my life verse: 'Then I heard the voice of the Lord saying, "Whom shall I send? And who will go for us?" And I said, "Here am I. Send me!"

When Rachel returned the next day, Louisa immediately brought out her Bible and asked Rachel to read. Afterward Rachel surprised her with a Spanish/English Bible and asked her to read in English. Louisa caressed her new Bible and turned to her favorite scriptures, reading aloud. She said she had loved the Lord all her life and didn't remember not loving Him. Rachel revealed her biggest regret was that she had not lived all her life for the Lord. They prayed together and she asked God to give Rachel another forty years to spend in service to Him.

Robert, Rachel and other team members visited El Moro, a fort built centuries ago to guard the entrance to the Havana harbor. They talked with men whose job was to raise the flag of a country whenever a ship from that country entered the harbor. One of the men was the last to raise the American flag in 1963. He showed them the cubicle still holding the American flag and said they long for the day when once again they will raise it, welcoming American ships.

We also visited the hospitals bringing medicine, beanie babies and Spanish New Testaments. When we asked if we were allowed to give out the Bibles, we were told: "Of course. We have religious freedom here." As we walked through the wards everyone wanted Bibles and many asked for prayer.

Less than a year later we returned to Cuba with great anticipation. Oh. The thrill of returning! Back in Havana we united with old friends. Our reception in the streets and churches was warm and enthusiastic. On Sunday morning our team walked into a church where the service had been going on for an hour. They stopped the service and stood cheering and weeping as we were led to the front row seats reserved in anticipation of our arrival. The pastor called us forward and the whole church prayed over us, and I was asked to speak.

That evening we worshiped in the beautiful church we had helped construct. Our friends were excited and proud to show us around. Rachel wanted to see Louisa and to give her a beautiful, black velvet jacket. Knowing she would be stunning in it she could not wait to see her wear it. When Rachel arrived at her house, her daughter said she was asleep but she would wake her. Rachel hesitated. She knew the team would be waiting. The service had been long and we needed to go back to our hotel. "Oh. Please do not wake her. Tell her I was here and I have a gift for her. I'll return next week."

Monday morning found us at our favorite hospital where we were told to come back later in the afternoon. There was a different feel when we were finally allowed in and presented the medicine to a guarded delegation of medical staff. A government official was present carrying a black notebook and taking notes and the staff appeared to be intimidated by his presence. We were permitted to visit the children and gave them beanie babies with the ever present official. We did not have any Bibles this time but passed out little booklets "Quien es Dios?" (Who is God?). If someone requested prayer we prayed. After all, we had been told Cuba has religious freedom.

The next morning we waited expectantly for our bus to take us to Cienfuego to spend a few days with other churches and hospitals. Those of us who'd been to Cienfuego could not wait to share it with our team members who were in Cuba for the first time. We chattered excitedly about special people we had met and poverty-stricken villages we had visited. "Just wait!" we kept saying. "The best is yet to come." Oh. And that church in the fishing village that was so rustic with no floors or windows… A church in Seattle sent money so they could complete construction. We could not wait to see it and to send pictures back to Seattle.

With us were three Cuban friends, Juan, Maria and Mario would serve as our interpreter/guides. They had been with us last year and were delighted to be going again.

Our bus was not arriving. I made phone call after phone call and after several hours of getting the runaround was finally told: "Everything is cancelled. You are asked to leave Cuba immediately because of your religious activity." We were stunned. We cried. Our Cuban friends cried.

Why? When we loved Cuba so much? We had done less this time than we had done last year. We thought there was religious freedom here. They have so many churches. Last year we had freely given out Bibles and Christian literature. Now they were sending vans to take us to the airport. We were no longer welcome in our beloved Cuba.

I called my powerful pastor friend. Maybe he could help. He was vague and evasive and not wanting to cause any hardship for him as he had seen enough of prison and torture over the years. I hung up realizing nothing could be done. We had to leave Cuba. No one could help us.

We still had boxes of medicine, beanie babies, baseball shirts and caps to distribute. A church was waiting for us in Cienfuego. We were going to help them with construction. People were counting on us!

We were crushed but determined the mission would not be defeated. It was just going to be different than we had planned. We knew the Creator of the Universe was in charge of this too. Quickly we loaded our supplies into the church van and Joshua, the driver, promised to take them to a safe place.

Rachel asked our remaining Cuban friends if they would be in trouble with the government after we had gone and they said not to worry. They would be okay. We gathered around them and prayed for their safety and strength for what was ahead. Then Juan said, "Now, let me pray for you." I believe that is when the women lost what remained of their makeup and the guys were no longer able to choke back tears.

Rachel's thoughts turned to Louisa. Why hadn't she allowed her daughter to wake her? Why didn't she linger there a few more moments to see her and give her the velvet jacket? She probably would never see her again. She went to her suitcase and tenderly held the jacket that she would never see her wear. Sobbing, she handed it to Juan, who knew her well. "Please give this to Louisa. Tell her I'm so sorry I couldn't give it to her myself. I love her and pray for her all the time. I'll see her next time I am allowed back to Cuba, or I'll see her in Heaven where we will all be free."

Maria kept pounding her fist on the table and spewing her anger. The guys kept shushing her. "You don't know who is watching and you don't want to get into trouble."

"I don't care! I'm tired of this dictatorship!"

"Please. Maria…"

Stunned, Rachel wondered, *Why can't Maria say out loud she is angry?* Patting her heart with her hand she addressed Maria: "They can't take away what we have here. If they don't allow us to return to Cuba, let's make an agreement to meet at the East Gate in Heaven in one million years."

"That is too long!" She slammed her fist onto the table.

Rachel reminded her that 1000 years is as one day with the Lord. "And I'm quite sure when I stand before my Jesus, I will fall face down and remain that way for at least a million years. Then if I'm able I'll get up and ask: 'Where's my mom? Where's Dad? Where are my family and friends?'"

Finally Maria agreed and the two of them made *un pacto* to meet at the East Gate of Heaven in one million years. As they clung to one another, heartbroken, they kept saying "Recuerda el pacto" (Remember the agreement).

Three vans arrived to take us to the airport. We were to fly to Cancun, Mexico. We were not sure what was really going to happen. Rachel took her memory stick from her camera and slid it into her pocket. *If they take the camera, at least I'll have my precious pictures.*

We boarded the vans with heavy hearts. Rachel was in the front seat of the third van and watched as the first two vans went straight, and her stem oversized driver took a left. *Oh my gosh! Why did we turn? Are they splitting us up? Are they taking us to the country to interrogate us?*

Timidly she glanced at the driver. He stared straight ahead, jaw set. She could not think of a word to say. Silently she called out to God, "I don't know where we are going but you do, so go with us!" *I should try to talk to the driver. I want him to know how much we love Cuba.* No words came.

Finally he slipped a tape into the tape deck, and as the music came forth Rachel attempted a smile and told him in Spanish, "I love Cuban music." He smiled back and started conversing in Spanish. *Uh oh. What if I can't keep up? My Spanish is far from fluent!* She stumbled through a conversation on Cuban music. She told him we had been to the Hotel Nacional and saw the Buena Vista Social Club and how thrilled she had been to sit at the feet of Compay Segundo.

He asked how long she had been in Cuba. When she told him only a few days he said: "You should stay longer. You haven't seen our beautiful beaches."

Nodding, she realized he was not even aware we were being deported. He was just doing his job of driving the van. She sat back and breathed normally when she saw a sign pointing to the airport. He knew a shortcut!

At the airport we were told our plane was boarding and it was impossible for us to embark, so I made more phone calls. The vans returned and took us to a hotel in downtown Havana where we would remain until the next afternoon.

Our spirits soared at the chance to spend one more night in our Cuba. We walked to the Hotel Nacional for dinner, thanking God for giving us a little more time to stroll the streets and waterfront of Havana. We breathed deeply as though we thought we could inhale a part of Cuba to take with us. There were always people in the streets. We didn't want to go inside our hotel. We wanted to experience it all just once more.

The next morning Rachel and Robert were on the streets early and met up with other team members at a French bakery. They stood on a corner watching all the activities and ate the best éclairs they had ever eaten. An old woman came up begging for coffee money so they gave her a dollar for coffee and two éclairs to go with it.

They rented coco car taxis which are like scooters with an open shell. There is enough room for two or three people to sit in the back seat. Their drivers were competitive and they raced through Havana carefree and laughing and at times grabbing on rather tightly. In Old Havana they peaked into a bar where Hemmingway drank away many hours with his friends. They stopped in a doorway to watch children playing in their classroom. They visited an old church and a museum. They sat on stairwells with old women who smoked big cigars. They reverently fingered old books in the open market. They talked with locals. A man offered himself as a guide and the police chased him away. When the police left he reappeared and angrily spat out, "If you are Cuban you have no rights! Only foreigners are free here." Rachel and Robert didn't comment.

Recently we learned Joshua, our Cuban driver, was living in the United States. He arrived hidden in the bottom of a boat where he and a number of other refugees huddled together for twelve hours not daring to move until they safely reached the shores of the United States. We met up with Joshua and asked what happened after he had driven away with our van full of supplies. He said he hid the van and was able to slowly and safely deliver all the gifts into the hands of those intended to receive them. The Cuban officials harassed him and followed him for quite some time after our expulsion and even offered him a prominent government position if he would turn in other Christians. When he refused, they stepped up the persecution until finally he found a route of escape and is loving the freedom he found here in the United States.

Our experiences in Cuba were a reminder to all of us that freedom is a remarkable gift. We realized the Christians in Cuba are risking everything to reach people for Christ. It inspires me to do even more to bring the message of hope that Christ offers. No person apart from Jesus has shaped the history of Christianity like the Apostle Paul. Even before he was a believer his actions were significant. His frenzied persecutions of Christians earned him a reputation of a man to be feared. After Paul met the Savior, all that intensity and passion was channeled into carrying the Good News to the world. Paul wrote:

> I have worked much harder, been in prison more frequently, been flogged more severely, and been exposed to death again and again. Five times I received from the Jews the forty lashes minus one. Three times I was beaten with rods, once I was stoned, three times I was shipwrecked, I spent a night and a day in the open sea, I have been constantly on the move. I have been in danger from rivers, in danger from bandits, in danger from my own countrymen, in danger from Gentiles; in danger in the city, in danger in the country, in danger at sea; and in danger from false brothers. I have labored and toiled and have often gone without sleep; I have known hunger and thirst and have often gone without food; I have been cold and naked. (2 Corinthians 11:23-27)

Oh to have that burning passion; to face all that for the cause of Christ!

Often I wonder why so much is demanded of followers of Christ who seem to have so little and are living in restricted nations. We in the States have so much and are free and we seem to have so little demanded of us by Jesus. While it appears we do not have much required of us, the Bible says, "From everyone who has been **given much, much** will be demanded; and from the one who has been entrusted with **much, much** more will be asked" (Luke 12:48 Author's emphasis).

When we are asked why we take medicine, shoes and toys to kids, we respond by saying, "We have been given so much. It is out of abundance and the mercy and grace of our Savior, Jesus Christ that we aspire to be giving, merciful and gracious to those in need."

"He has showed you, O man, what is good. And what does the Lord require of you? To act justly and to love mercy and to walk humbly with your God" (Micah 6:8).

Dad and Mom at Pilot Knob

Mom and Dad with
granddaughter Lisa

Brothers Ricky and Tommy

Rachel on the far right
and her sisters at Migrant Camp

Mom and Flo on the porch

Cuba—Company Segundo

Cuba—Girl in hospital
admires Tom

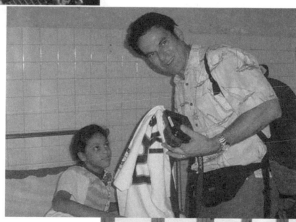

Cuba—Louisa and Rachel

Cuba—Medicine for Cuba

Cuba–Showing American flag at Havana Port of Entry

Cuba–Tom in Cuban village

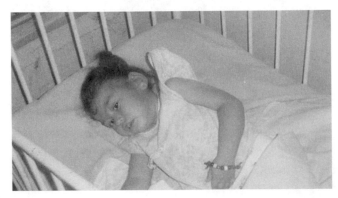

Cuban hospital

Peru—barrio

Peru—Tom with
children in barrio

Peru—house in barrio

Peru—house in barrio

Peru—Children in the barrio

Romania—Children with Tom

Romania—Mishu distributing gifts
in gypsy village

Romania—Pamela lives in a gypsy village

Russia—Robert and Rachel at Summer Palace near St. Petersburg

Russia—Tchaikovsky grave - Ramona, Rachel, Tom

Russia—Team with Sasha in St. Petersburg

Russia—Tom at Museum
of Atheism

Russia—Tom, Sasha, Rachel

Russia—women

Uganda—dedication of hospital
built by H4K1

Uganda—Colleen prays with Cadija

Uganda—church built by Christ Church of the Valley

Uganda—Grace
and her children

Uganda—H4K1 team

Uganda—hospital built by
H4K1 Supporters

Uganda—in the bush

Uganda—Issa

Uganda—medical supplies
carried by H4K1 team

Uganda—Pastor Chris and Robert

Uganda—Pastor Justis and Robert

Uganda–Pastor Peter's new Church built by fellowship Anthem

Uganda–Pastor Peter's new Church built by fellowship Anthem

Uganda–Pastor Ruth and Tom

Uganda–Pastor Ruth with
Karamojong tribe

Uganda—Rachel and baby Rachel

Uganda—Rachel and sponsored children

Uganda—Rachel and Tom at the Equator

Uganda—Rachel with 2nd and 3rd generations

Uganda—Rachel's granddaughter greets children

Uganda—sharing a plate of food

Uganda—Tom at hospital
dedication

Uganda—Tom with American and
Ugandan children

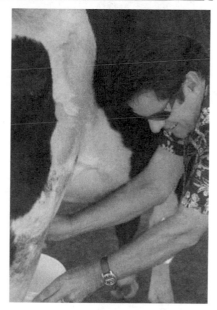

Uganda—Tom milking a cow

Uganda—watching Oprah on one
of the very few TV sets

Uganda—Wazemba cooking
in her hut

Uganda—worried children

Uganda—orphans

Chapter Five

Journeys of Mercy

y life appeared to be perfect. I was on top and invited to speak in prestigious churches, conferences and events throughout the world. I knew important people and considered myself to be one of them. My international short term mission teams were flourishing. I was the mission director at a mega-church in Phoenix. I had a beautiful home, had been married twenty-two years and had three fantastic children. "You rebuke the arrogant, who are cursed and stray from your commands" (Psalm 119:21).

Suddenly my world came crashing down. "I am laid low in the dust; presere my life according to your word" (Psalm 119:25). While the outside was looking good, inside I was in immense pain. For years my marriage had been disintegrating and we had grown miles apart, spending days and weeks in silence. As our animosity toward one another grew, we coped by putting our lives into our separate careers. Our kids were growing up in an environment with parents who never expressed affection or love for one another. The pressure to keep this hidden because of my public ministry led us to internalize the pain and to live a life of lies. In the mid-nineties when we could no longer reside in this destructive life, we decided my wife would move out and I would remain in the home with our three children.

"My soul is weary with sorrow; strengthen me according to your word" (Psalm 119:28). The anguish of coming face to face with problems that had been pushed beneath the surface all those years was crushing. I had an overwhelming sense of failure. In the past I had been highly critical of Christians divorcing. Now I was in the same category and my shame was multiplied knowing it would lower the standard of which I had always held high for a Christian.

I sank into a deep depression. Physically and emotionally exhausted I tried to keep the house spotless. I focused on ironing, mopping floors and trying to have meals ready on time while juggling the kids' schedules.

The pain accelerated as more and more people heard of my divorce. I received phone call after phone call canceling my speaking engagements. Many people were hurt and angry and quick to condemn. I was told things like: "If you can't save your own marriage you have no business being in Christian ministry. Your ministry is over." I remembered reading a book a number of years ago, *Please Don't Shoot, I'm Already Wounded.* The author stated, "The Evangelicals are the only group who shoot their wounded." And, "The most lonely place for a divorced person to be is in the church."[7] Wow! Did I ever find that to be true as poisoned arrow after arrow came aimed at my heart. I wondered, *Are these true followers of Jesus Christ or are they the religious people? Had I become one of those religious people?*

Is there hope? I continually asked myself. "May your unfailing love come to me, O Lord, your salvation according to your promise" (Psalm 119:41). Because churches and religious organizations had cancelled my speaking engagements, I was left financially devastated. I borrowed money to pay bills. Frequently I withdrew to my darkened bedroom and wept bitterly. I did not need others to condemn me as I was doing a pretty good job of that myself. I wanted to die and to escape the pain. My pastor and counselor told me, "Tom, you have to accept God's mercy on you." My background of trying to keep the rules and earning God's love kept haunting me. I could not accept His unconditional mercy and forgiveness.

"Remember your word to your servant, for you have given me hope" (Psalm 119:49). One morning after jogging I sat on my patio to cool down. I was as low as I had ever been. I could not grasp that God wanted to show His love and mercy toward me, and I believed I deserved His wrath and punishment. I hung my head and grieved. As I sat with my head between my hands and elbows propped on my knees, I became aware of my dog. He rested his head on my feet, gazed at me through loving eyes and continually wagged his tail. In that moment, in the depth of depression, God chose to show me an example of His unconditional love through my dog, Buddy. Hope began to grow. *If an animal can show this kind of unconditional love, how much more does my Creator love me?* My tears flowed faster now as relief flooded through me. My God cared about my pain. He saw how the religious people had hurt me and was using it to change me. I remembered my friend Natasha thanking God for her struggles "because they make us strong."

Not long afterward I was called to the home of a friend who was dying of cancer. I sat beside his bed and took his hand. "Tom," he said, "Tell me about your divorce. Tell me what happened." I poured my heart out, describing the years of hiding behind my religious mask of self-righteousness. I told him about the guilt, the rejection by religious people, and the devastation of my ministry. I told him how I had discovered God's mercy and forgiveness.

When I finished he said: "Thank you for your honesty. Now I can be honest with you and tell you the truth of my life. I am not the person the people in my church think I am. I have given millions to my church for the approval of man. I have done so many things wrong in my life that I am afraid to die. I don't believe I am going to Heaven because I'm not good enough." Over the next minutes I listened as this respected elder of the church poured out a confession of sin. We prayed together. When we finished, he said, "Now I have peace." He died the next week. I knew if I had not been straightforward about the horrible ordeal of my divorce, he would never have trusted me with his secret and may not have gotten things right with God.

As I continued to heal, I prayed; "God, the religious people might never accept me because of my failure. Send me to those in need. Send me to those who have no hope. Use me if You will."

Diane Brask who is currently working in the slums of Kampala, Uganda told me: "The religious people probably won't want to hear from you, but you weren't called to the religious. You were called to the hurting, and a hurting kid isn't going to ask you if you've been divorced."

"My comfort in my suffering is this: Your promise preserves my life" (Psalm 119:50). I reflected on an experience I had had in Bible school after first turning my life over to Christ. I was discouraged and was not sure I could live the Christian life and was ready to walk away from God. One weekend I left school and spent the weekend getting high, knowing I would be kicked out of school if anyone found out. Monday morning when I was called into the president's office, I was sure someone had told and I was finished with Bible school. I slumped in my chair waiting for the lecture. Dr. Force said: "Tom. I know you had a difficult weekend. I don't want to know what you've done. I just want you to know I've not been able to get you off my mind. I have been praying for you all weekend. Whatever it was you were struggling with is forgiven. I will pray for you and I want you to pray for me."

I protested about praying for him because he was such a good Christian, and I was just a worm. Dr Force assured me: "The ground at the foot of the cross is level. It takes the same grace to forgive me every day as it does for you."

Remembering those words I began to focus on the cross. Jesus had paid for my failures and sin. I was justified! There was no rule I could follow, no life I could lead that would be good enough to enter Heaven. I needed and accepted the forgiveness that Jesus offered when he died in my place. I saw myself as a fragile sinful human. The only hope I had was His mercy and grace. I was changing. My faith was no longer built on my image but on His overwhelming love. The gospel really is the Good News!

Everyday I thank Him for His mercy on me. It is all I have.

A number of months later, Sarah who is now my wife came into my life. Her incredible honesty and ability to communicate brought a deeper healing. I opened up and began to tell her things of which I had never spoken. We became great friends, and through remarkable conversations and praying together, we found we had a similar heart to bring hope to the hurting. Today she is my best friend. We have two children together, and not only is she a loving mother but she is supportive of all that I do. When I came back from Africa for the first time, she said, "A part of your heart is still in Africa. As much as I miss you when you are away, you have to go back."

After my ordeal of judging and being judged, I prayed to look at others in a different light. Max Lucado, in his book, *In the Grip of Grace*, tells us we have no right to judge anyone.

> Not only are we unworthy, we are unqualified. We don't know enough about the person to judge him. We don't know enough about his past. We condemn a man for stumbling this morning, but we didn't see the blows he took yesterday. We judge a woman for the limp in her walk but cannot see the tack in her shoe. We mock the fear in their eyes but have no idea how many stones they have ducked or darts they have dodged.[8]

I want to reflect God's mercy in all that I do. My desire is not to be religious but to be like Jesus. Though Jesus was the holiest, most perfect, Godly person to live without sin, sinners flocked to him. What was it about Him that had the outcasts of society following Him wherever He went? I believe it was His nonjudgmental attitude toward those who were in distress.

I love the story in John, chapter eight, of the religious leaders bringing the prostitute before Jesus. I imagine them roughly thrusting her toward Him, their disdain for her written all over their faces, their body language and scornful words. "Teacher, this woman was caught in the act of adultery. In the Law Moses commanded us to stone such women. Now what do you say (vv. 4-5)? Jesus did not answer. Instead he knelt down and began writing in the dirt. Some scholars say he was writing words like liar, *thief, extortioner.* Then Jesus stood up and looked at the religious leaders. I like to think he had eye contact with each of them before saying: "If any one of you is without sin, let him be the first to throw a stone at her."

Again Jesus knelt and wrote in the dirt. Perhaps he wrote things like *gluttony, fornicator,* and *hypocrite.* One by one the religious men silently slipped away. Jesus stood and asked the woman: "Woman, where are they? Has no one condemned you?"

"No one, sir," she said.

"Then neither do I condemn you," Jesus declared. "Go now and leave your life of sin" (vv. 10-11).

A few years ago I led a team to Romania. One of our projects was to set up a medical and dental clinic in partnership with a local Christian organization.

Liz, a nurse from California and an Australian girl, Min were singing and playing a guitar in their hotel room. Maria, a young gypsy prostitute heard them and appeared at their door. To their delight, Maria asked if she could join them. They laughed and sang together and Maria treated them by singing a gypsy song. During the course of the evening, the two girls told Maria they were Christians. She responded sadly: "Christians hate me. I'm a prostitute." Min and Liz assured her that they loved her just as she was and more importantly so did Jesus. They asked her if she would like to help set up the medical clinic the next day. She happily agreed.

When the Romanian director, George and his wife saw Maria they called me aside. "That girl cannot be here."

"Why not?"

"She's a gypsy. They are lower than parasites."

"But this clinic is for everyone," I argued.

"We don't want her."

I couldn't believe what these Christians were saying to me! "We represent Jesus. Our arms are open to everyone."

"Jesus doesn't want these kind of people!"

Shocked, I responded; "Really? Well, I'm here and you're here...."

They were unrelenting and coldly sent Maria away.

Our team was crushed and angry. They were ready to pack it up and leave. I urged them to pray and not let it destroy what we were trying to do. We treated people for two days, praying all the while.

The second day George and his wife approached me. "We haven't been able to sleep."

Good!

"We've made a mistake. We were wrong to send that girl away. We should treat gypsies too."

Liz did manage to catch up with Maria at the hotel. She apologized and told her how grieved she was that a Christian would treat her so badly. She prayed with her and gave her a Bible.

Does not the potter have the right to make out of the same lump of clay some pottery for noble purposes and some for common use? What if God, choosing to show his wrath and make his power known, bore with great patience the objects of his wrath— prepared for destruction? What if he did this to make the riches of his glory known to the objects of his mercy, whom he prepared in advance for glory—even us, whom he also called, not only from the Jews but also from the Gentiles? (Romans 9:21-24)

We deserve to be judged, but because of the cross we have received mercy. It is as though we have never sinned! I believe as Christians we are to reflect His mercy in all that we do and say. We are given many opportunities. It is up to us to use, recognize them and to become His vessel of mercy.

Days ago I was in Romania with a team doing outreach work with the gypsy villages. While the team enjoyed the city of Clug, I wandered off to find a place to eat. A man tapped me on the shoulder. It was George! He was on his way to pay his electric bill, and he saw me out of the corner of his eye. It had been five years since George decided to treat gypsies at his clinic, and here in a town of about a half of a million people we happened across one another. We greeted one another joyfully, and I asked how the clinic was doing, and George replied it was doing well, staying busy, but that was not his main focus anymore. His main ministry is to the Gypsies. He had a new love for the Gypsies and an urgency to help them.

One winter I took a team to a homeless shelter in Chillan, Chile. Pat, our board chairman, played his clarinet, filling the dismal shelter with music. Others danced with the men. The place filled with laughter and joy as we hugged the men and gave them clothing and served a hot meal. Noticing their need for blankets, we slipped out and bought some. I saw a man wearing sandals with no socks. I thought of my warm socks and knew his feet were cold. I looked at his filthy, smelly, broken and bleeding feet and considered God's mercy toward me. I had no choice. I took off my socks and kneeling at his feet, put them on him. What a privilege to experience Christ's goodness and mercy.

Our family has experienced God's mercy many times. Rachel and Robert bought a summer home in Iowa. The plan was to be near our mom at least part of the year. Mom and Rachel had many plans.

Robert didn't like Iowa winters but loved the summers, so every winter Rachel would fly home alone to spend time with Mom and play in the snow with our niece's kids. At night she enjoyed wrapping up in an afghan and drinking tea while she and Mom talked and listened to the wind howling, rattling the windows of our old house. Rachel thought it was fun to sleep in her old room and write in the frost that formed on her upstairs window. She would mull over childhood memories and wake to the smell of banana bread baking.

Although Mom was nearing eighty, she didn't mind taking her big Cadillac out onto snowy roads to go shopping in Mason City or to have a cinnamon roll at the Red Owl in Forest City. She knew all the fun craft and antique shops and they would spend hours browsing for treasures.

Rachel and Mom decided when Robert retired they should buy a summer home in Iowa. Our nephew, Dan, helped Rachel find a fabulous two-storybuilt in the 1920s. It had a nice, open front porch where Rachel visualized having coffee with Mom and all her family and friends. Robert agreed and they bought the house.

The day they moved some of their things from Arizona, Mom was there. She had a doctor's appointment, but she said it wasn't important. She would rather watch Rachel unpack.

They chatted as Rachel set up the kitchen and unwrapped her vintage and antique glass ware. Mom would admire a piece and Rachel would give it to her. They talked about plans for her eightieth birthday party which was just a few weeks away.

All six of our brothers and sisters and most of their families were going to be there. Our aunt and uncle from Indiana and many relatives in the area would be attending our two-day party. Our brother, Rick and his daughter, Tati, were coming home from Chile. We had a lot to do.

Mom didn't look good and complained of lower back and leg pain. Not one to be depressed, she appeared to be now. We watched our strong, independent mom become whiney and needy. We thought maybe the excitement was too much and after the party she would be better. She was not.

Rick stayed with her for several weeks. Realizing she could no longer live alone, he talked her into moving into a senior living complex. She had a beautiful apartment and had the option of going to the common dining room for meals. She loved her new place, but her health continued to decline.

Her doctor sent her to an oncologist after running tests. Rachel took her. The oncologist said, "I'm a cancer doctor. Do you know why you're here?"

"I suppose it has something to do with the spots on my lungs, but that's not cancer. They've always been there. Thirty years ago I had cervical and colon cancer."

"Yes. I know. I read your chart and all the doctors wrote things like 'This woman will not make it' or 'This woman will not live more than six months.'"

Rachel nodded. "We've been so blessed to have her all these years and are grateful that God extended her life."

"Well," the doctor took Mom's hand. "I'm sorry to tell you you have lung and stomach cancer and there is nothing we can do for you."

Rachel froze. Mom didn't seem fazed by his words.

He talked about blood transfusions, and Rachel honestly does not remember why they were going to do that. Mom seemed to think that would be her treatment and went along with it.

Rachel tried to hold herself together and cheerfully wheeled Mom to the lab for blood work. Then she went back to the doctor and started asking questions. He said Mom had six months at the very most.

A few days later Mom was hospitalized and this time the news sank in. My sisters walked into her hospital room and she blurted through tears, "I'm going to my Heavenly home. There is nothing they can do."

They all erupted into tears and held onto one another. All those plans....

The next day with the help of Hospice, Mom moved into Rachel and Robert's summer home. Robert, Joan, Ramona and Rachel doted on her. If she wanted something they tore the house apart to get it. One night she wanted applesauce. Rachel didn't have any but she had her homemade apple butter. She spooned it into a dish and hoped it would satisfy Mom. "This is the best applesauce I've ever had," she announced as she held out the dish and asked for more.

When our sister, Judy, arrived Mom said, "Oh good. Finally someone who knows how to cook." Our nephew, Dan, and our nieces, Beth and Melanie came by daily to see Grandma. It turned out to be a special time as family and friends constantly were dropping by. Those who were not able to travel to Iowa called her often to say, "I love you."

Rachel's favorite photo is of Mom and her friend Flo sitting on the front porch, eyes locked as they talked. Joan and Rachel sneaked around the outside of the house and snapped pictures. What they talked about we don't know. What do old friends say when one is dying? Did Mom talk about dying or did they talk about the weather, their kids and everyday things? Rachel was so moved watching them that she later remarked to her friend, Wendy Hopkins, "I hope when I'm dying I have at least one good friend to sit on the porch with me."

She and Joan said, "We'll come and sit on the porch with you."

Later Wendy returned with another friend, Jane, and said, "We don't have to wait till you're dying to sit on the porch." So the three of them sat on the steps and didn't say much. Every once in a while Wendy would put an arm around Rachel's shoulder and squeeze. Rachel studied a crack in the steps and blinked back tears. She understood then it did not matter what Mom and Flo said to one another. It must have been comforting just to sit together.

I was in Chile leading a mission team. Sarah called to tell me Mom was deteriorating quickly. I wanted to come home, but when I talked to Mom by phone she said she would wait for me and to finish the mission.

My sisters were praying she would be able to hang on. They played Gaither gospel CDs softly in her room to comfort her. One evening Rachel remarked to a visitor that Mom had been in a deep sleep for quite a while. The visitor looked at her and said maybe she was in a diabetic coma so they called the hospice nurse. She confirmed it and said: "She's in a peaceful state. We can just let her go and she won't be in any pain."

Sobbing uncontrollably, Rachel wailed: "You have to wake her! My brother is coming and wants to say goodbye. She promised she'd wait for him!"

The nurse said she would try, and although it was a real struggle she brought Mom out of the coma. My sisters watched her closely until finally Sarah and I arrived. She was so happy to see us. I sat alone with her with the door closed for a long while. I held her hand, prayed for her and wept. Mom had declined so much since her party it was shocking to see her. I sat watching her, thinking about her life and the impact she had had on my life. She had always been a woman of adventure. When she was seventeen, she secretly took flying lessons then coaxed her dad to the airport where she announced she was ready to take a solo flight and had him watch!

She was a writer and during her child-rearing years most of her escapades took place at the typewriter. Now she was facing death with the same courage she had lived her life.

That evening family and friends gathered around Mom's bed. Our dear friend, Lucille Skogen, suggested we sing hymns. Mom smiled and drifted in and out as we sang every hymn we could think of.

Ramona stood next to the bed crying. Mom opened her eyes. "Ah, don't cry." She reached up and gently wiped Ramona's tears.

We started singing praise songs and were sure we were going to sing her right into the arms of Jesus, but she thought she would like a piece of Robert's birthday cake first.

Those next days were quiet and sweet. One morning Rachel walked into Mom's room and caught her staring at nothing. She raised her hand and pointed. "How do you measure that?" *She sees heaven!* She turned and said, "Oh, good morning, Gary." Gary was my nephew who had been murdered when he was thirteen. *Oh my gosh! She saw Gary!*

Rachel sat next to her kissing her hand then picked up her Bible and began reading aloud.

> The angel who talked with me had a measuring rod of gold to measure the city, its gates and its walls . . . The wall was made of jasper, and the city of pure gold, as pure as glass. The foundations of the city walls were decorated with every kind of precious stone. The twelve gates were twelve pearls, each gate made of a single pearl. The great street of the city was of pure gold, like transparent glass. I did not see a temple in the city, because the Lord God Almighty and the Lamb are its temple. The city does not need the

sun or the moon to shine on it, for the glory of God gives it light, and the Lamb is its lamp. The nations will walk by its light, and the kings of the earth will bring their splendor into it. On no day will its gates ever be shut, for there will be no night there. The glory and honor of the nations will be brought into it. Nothing impure will ever enter it, nor will anyone who does what is shameful or deceitful, but only those whose names are written in the Lamb's book of life." (Rev 21:15-27)

Setting her Bible aside Rachel watched Mom sleep. There were so many things she wanted to say. Then maybe she had already said them. Mom opened her eyes and asked about Rachel's daughter, Lisa and grand-daughter, Jordan. Rachel filled her in on the latest news. "You're a good mother," Mom said. "I wasn't a very good mother."

Rachel clutched her hand and held it against her cheek. "That's not true. I learned so much from you—where I get my free spirit. You were a great mom. Remember when you let me paint my bedroom ceiling and trim bright red? I even painted the light bulb!" Mom smiled and floated off again. Rachel thought about her daughter and how she was always apologizing for being a lousy mother, and Lisa denies it and tells her she was the best. I wonder if all mothers feel like they have failed their daughters somehow.

My sister Marty and Rachel made a memory book for Mom's eightieth. Family members and friends all contributed notes and pictures. Mom cherished it and kept in next to her bed. Rachel picked it up and started flipping through the pages.

Rick had written: "Madre was always there. Before, during and after school. You could always count on her. She would make some hot bread for us when we came home. I always remember Madre washing clothes and doing dishes. Seems like this was a never ending job. Thanks, Madre, for all the little things you did and do that we never realized. Thanks for the sacrifices you made. You've been a great, Madre. Although I almost never use the word, I want you to know I love you, Madre. Like they say—if I tell you once, I do not need to say it again unless the situation changes, then I'll let you know."

Rachel smiled and shook her head. *Rick. He's such a sweetie. He shows love in everything he does. He's just a little awkward about saying he loves you. Whenever I say, "I love you!" he says, "Yah. Okay."*

Turning the page Rachel read a poem Joan wrote when she was nine years old. "My mother is so nice. / She's as lovely as rice. / Although she doesn't like mice, / I'd never give her away for any price." *Hmmm. And they think I'm the writer!*

I wrote: "There are so many memories of your strength in standing up for us kids. One that stands out is when a school teacher stopped and yelled at us kids for shouting, "Lefty" at him. We hid behind your skirts and you called him a louse. Many times you went up to the school to defend me. Thanks! Your passion for the Mexican migrant workers was a great example for me and my future ministry. It was great when you bought the plastic record player to play the gospel in Spanish. Your acceptance of people without prejudice lives on through your kids. Thank you for inspiring and passing the legacy of living for Christ, not just in word, but in action. I love you, Mom."

Rachel chuckled. *Oh yeah. She stuck up for me a number of times too. I wanted to be a hippie, and she was so used to teenagers by the time I became one that my mini-skirts, hairstyles and attitude didn't faze her, and she was quick to defend me to anyone who was critical.* She caressed her cheek with Mom's hand and whispered, "Yes. You were a great mom!"

Mom stirred and tried to sit up. Quickly Rachel jumped up and adjusted her bed and pillows. Robert walked in with a plate of food. "Judy made goulash. Do you want some?" He sat down and began to feed her. Rachel left them to chitchat and carried the memory book to the living room where she continued to page through it reading all the entries. She marveled at how many mentioned Mom's faith and her Christian influence on us all.

Her eyes fell on the entry from her daughter, Lisa:

*Dear Grandma, I just wanted to share with you some of my wonderful
memories I have of growing up around you. I remember picking violets
from your yard before you mowed, snapping beans, working side by
side with you in your garden, watching you put on lipstick before playing piano at Temple Baptist, teaching my Sunday School class.
Remember when we lived in the house next door to you, and every
morning you'd make a big pot of oatmeal for my dog Muffy? I remember watching Lawrence Welk with you and Grandpa. I remember your
homemade macaroni and cheese, the Salisbury steak TV dinners, and
that your freezer was always filled with angel food cake slices. When
we went to bed, you would always stay up writing in your notebooks
or reading. Remember when we used to take naps every afternoon, and
then at three o'clock we'd get up and you and Grandpa and I would all
have bowls of ice cream with powdered Nestle's Quick? Thanks for all
the great memories. Happy eightieth!*

Closing the book Rachel considered the legacy Mom was leaving. Her
kids, grandkids and great-grandkids all have knowledge of her faith in
God and a number of us are in some type of part-time or full-time service. Rachel remembered an email Joan received from her son, Mark.

*Take care of my grammy. We just cherish and love her more than words
can describe. But we aren't worried about her. Jesus is going to take
good care of her. If she goes today or in ten years she will wind up in
the same place...in big Papa's arms and she'll dance around and drink
coffee with Lutherans... Let her know she should save me a place next
to her because I want to hang out and chat with her for one-and-a-half
million years or so.*

Our theme song was *Holy Ground.* It was on one of the Gaither CDs
and whenever it came on, we would turn it up a little and sing along. I
imagined the angels standing in the wings waiting for Mom putting their
hands over their ears as we lifted our not so musical voices. We were so

grateful that God had given us this time with Mom and thought about how many people do not get the chance to say goodbye to their loved ones. God had been merciful throughout Mom's short illness and now her death.

On the evening of August 15, 2001 I decided to bake cookies. We all were busy around the house. We had been told by hospice that when the end comes, Mom would breathe like a fish out of water. Rachel stopped by her open doorway and saw her breathing in that manner and quickly called the others. As we gathered around her bed, Judy said, "Listen! That song is playing." She turned up the CD player and Holy Ground ushered Mom into eternity.

The words she requested on her tombstone read, "Meet me at the East Gate."

I will always be grateful for God's mercy in my mother's final days and how it all worked out so we could be with her and send her to eternity. I imagined Jesus standing on the shores beckoning to her to come on home. I imagined Him saying, "Well done, good and faithful servant" (Matthew 25:21).

Chapter Six

Riding Out the Storm

Just when it seems that life's final wave is about to crash down on you, God sends a lifeboat. I nearly died of food poisoning on one of my trips to China. I was so weak I could hardly find my way to a public restroom where the toilet is simply a hole in the floor and many are so filthy it is almost impossible to breathe. I stumbled into one, fell to the floor and began vomiting. Vaguely I remember someone coming in and asking if I needed help. I had Christian literature in my pockets and knew I would be in big trouble if it was found on me. Somehow I communicated this to the person and he dug in my pockets and disposed of the literature. As I wobbled in and out of consciousness, I hazily remember someone picking me off the floor and saying I was dying. I was carried to a bus and taken to the nearest hospital.

When I came to, I didn't know where I was. Repulsed by the rusty intravenous needle I saw sticking into my arm and the ants crawling in my bed, I began to remember the bathroom floor and realized I was in a Chinese hospital.

Later I was told the medical personnel were unable to detect a pulse when I was brought in. Deathly ill and half a world away from home, I struggled to rise above the waves that threatened to take my life. Why would God allow this to happen?

Grappling to retain consciousness, I realized I had not been alone as I fought through the night. Mr. Wong, a confirmed atheist, had debated the existence of God with me throughout our entire trip. There were times he vehemently told me I was a fool for believing in God. But that night Mr. Wong remained at my bedside placing a cool towel on my forehead to keep my fever down. I made an effort to thank him for his love and concern. "I thought I was going to die."

"Tom, you weren't going to die. I saw God with you."

Chuck was addicted to alcohol. One night while drinking in a local tavern in Lake Mills, Iowa, he became disruptive and was thrown out. Enraged he crashed his car into a tree. When he stumbled back to the tavern and found it had closed, he attempted to break down the door and threatened to kill the police officer who arrived on the scene. Unable to restrain Chuck, the officer called for backup, but by the time the other officer arrived Chuck was back in his car weaving toward home. They followed him and jumped him when he bolted from his car. Two officers and a great deal of mace finally subdued him enough to place him in jail.

Chuck's brother Leo and I were called to his jail cell at two o'clock in the morning. In those early morning hours God answered the years of prayer Chuck's family had uttered on his behalf. Leo and I knelt next to him with handkerchiefs covering our noses and mouths to filter the overpowering odor of the mace as Chuck asked Jesus to be Lord of his life. He was forever altered.

His reputation was known throughout the county of that rural area. Many people said religion would do him no good. He was too far gone. They were right. It was not religion but his relationship with Christ that shined through him, and many of his friends came to find hope in Jesus as a result of his testimony of a radically changed life. As he brought his friends to Christ and his business prospered, he used his resources to buy books and Bibles to give out and became a generous supporter of our ministry

It was the day after Christmas, and I was getting ready to move out of the cold snowy Iowa winters to Arizona. Chuck was working to finish a construction job so he could help me drive our truck full of furniture. He and his team were placing large, round drainage tile in a ditch. Chuck operated the machine to lower the tile while the bottom man guided the tile to its proper place. It was cold and wet. When the bottom man complained he had a hole in his boot and his feet were getting soaked, Chuck traded places. A 700-pound tile slipped from the grips of the machine and landed on him sending Chuck to eternity. He was fifty years old.

His Bible, which he read that morning, was still open to the fourteenth chapter of John. Jesus was telling His disciples He was leaving them:

> Do not let your hearts be troubled. Trust in God; trust also in me. In my Father's house are many rooms; if it were not so, I would have told you. I am going there to prepare a place for you. And if I go and prepare a place for you, I will come back and take you to be with me that you also may be where I am. You know the way to the place where I am going... Peace I leave with you; my peace I give you. I do not give to you as the world gives. Do not let your hearts be troubled and do not be afraid. (John 14:1-4, 27)

Chuck found peace in that jail cell and discovered what it meant to be free from the things that once ensnared him. He knew what it meant to be free to really love others as well as himself. Chuck knew Jesus.

I battled with Chuck's death. It seemed so unfair. Maybe I shouldn't have asked him to help with my move. Maybe he wouldn't have been rushing the job. Maybe he wouldn't have been working the day after Christmas.

Eventually I found reconciliation in the promise, "Peace I leave with

you; my peace I give to you." If the accident had happened a few years earlier, Chuck would not be with the Lord. He had been given a few years to
serve the Lord and did it well. I can almost see the Father inviting Chuck
through those gates of pearl saying; "Welcome home my son. Well done
you good and faithful servant."

Nothing breaks my heart faster than seeing an innocent child helplessly
lying in bed too sick to smile, hooked up to machines, being poked with
needles. Tears collect in my throat making vocalizations impossible when
I look into vulnerable eyes and know I can do nothing. I want to cry out,
"God! Where are you in this? Why do children have to suffer?" I have been
subjected to this over and over and it does not get any easier.

A number of years ago I took a team to a children's cancer hospital in
Russia where the survival rate was about fifteen percent. We brought medicine, medical supplies and beanie babies to hand out while we visited the
children. It was here David and Susan met little five-year-old Katya. Little
Katya had no family. Abandoned, she would die alone. A towel was
wrapped around her head covering her hairless scalp. Her body was covered with sores due to incorrect doses of chemo, yet her dark eyes danced
with laughter. Susan placed a picture of their family over Katya's bed. "We
are your family now."

When David and Susan returned to Montana, Katya weighed on their
hearts. We tell team members that adopting is impossible, and to adopt a
child you have chosen is even more impossible! Susan and David were
determined to try anyway. They took out a second mortgage on their
home and miraculously were able to adopt Katya who was so ill that her
initial trip had to be delayed until she was well enough to travel. Susan
and David took her to Seattle Children's hospital for radical chemo treatments. Her cancer went into remission.

What a joy she was to her new family. She accepted Christ as Savior
and truly lived a joyful, abundant life. I developed a close relationship

with her and visited her whenever I could. I will never forget speaking at her church when she was about seven years old. As I looked out during worship there she stood in the front row with her hands raised toward heaven, praising God. I smiled, watching her and remembering the first time I saw her so frail and sick and alone in that Russian hospital. Now here she was strong and full of life with a family who loved her heartily.

In November of 1999 the unthinkable happened. The cancer returned. Susan and David were told the cancer was in her central nervous system and the growth on her brain was spreading rapidly. I went to see her. I can still see her twinkling eyes beneath her little bald head. "I was at a wedding and danced the funky monkey."

"The funky monkey? Is that anything like the funky chicken?"

Joyfully she shrugged her shoulders. What a beautiful child she was. I wondered if this little girl so full of life knew how close to death she was.

Katya was receiving chemo and had lost her appetite. Her mom brought in a piece of apple pie. I teased, "I'm going to eat your apple pie."

"That's my pie!" Pretty soon she gobbled it down grinning the whole time.

We talked about Thanksgiving. I told her my favorite thing at Thanksgiving was mincemeat pie and asked what her favorite thing about Thanksgiving was. She smiled, eyes sparkling. "Family."

In January I was told Katya didn't have long to live. I went to see her for the last time. My wife, Sarah, was pregnant and I whispered the news to Katya. She was giggly over our secret and whispered back, "Maybe if it's a girl you could name her Katya." When her family came into the room she would taunt them. "I know something you don't know." It was unbelievable to me as sick as she was she still had such humor.

I was amazed at the number of lives Katya had touched. This delightful child who loved so much had next to her bed over 700 get well cards. We would read them together until she got tired and she would rest awhile. I watched her sleep and felt those tears welling up in my throat. "God, where *are* You?"

I know that when our hearts shatter His breaks too. I started thinking about the three years Katya had a family. This vibrant, outgoing, strong-willed child really lived a jam-packed life. She was confident that Jesus loved her and knew without a doubt that she was loved by her family. If this wonderful family had not rescued her, she would have died alone in a Russian hospital. She would not have known so much love and laughter. She would have died without her Savior.

It was February Katya would be going to her eternal home. Her father was lying in bed next to her, holding her, treasuring the short hours he had left with his precious little girl. She spoke. "Jesus was here. He touched my hand." Her father could not answer. He stroked her face and swallowed his tears. After a time of silence she spoke again. "Papa. The angels are here."

Clutching her a little tighter, he asked, "How many are there? Two? Three?"

"Papa. There are thousands!"

That night while her parents slept, Katya took her final breath and left with the angels.

A number of months later our daughter, Sophia Katya Eggum, was born.

We never know when we will be caught in the eye of a storm. Sometimes we are carried by the swell, experience the thrill and come out strong while others appear to have lost the battle. We serve a mighty God, and even when it seems hopeless, we know in the midst of the squall, He is there. We question. We beg. We cry. We even get angry with God. We try to understand yet for some things there is no explanation.

While in Croatia one night I stood on the white, rocky shoreline of the Adriatic Sea. The moon was full. The waves gently lapped at the shore creating a peaceful, postcard moment. Feeling refreshed in the moment, I realized sometimes life is like that. Everything is laid-back and life is good… All of a sudden out of nowhere a storm boils with rage. The sea that was so calm now churns violently. We can be destroyed by the upheaval and give up on life or grasp His lifeline and ride out the storm.

My breathing was heavier than it had been over the past years when I jogged to my favorite little creek in the countryside outside Frederick, Maryland. I knelt at the little bridge over Tuscarora Creek giving thanks to God for His protection over the countless events and miles I had traveled since I last visited this peaceful place. It was here I had received a fresh vision of how we could respond to the incredible need we had seen in Africa. Often I felt His peace and direction as I wept in prayer for my family and the purpose for which He had called me. I watched the cool water trickle over the moss covered rocks and reflected on the past eight months. Then I had seen the autumn leaves fill the creek banks with unbelievable colors and felt the crisp air of an October morning as I ran a four-mile trail through this refreshing landscape of weathered barns and rolling hills. Leaning over the bridge I watched the water swirl gently beneath me and reflected over the changes the past months had brought into my life.

Last December I reluctantly went in for a complete physical. Usually I am energetic and require little sleep. I had been feeling that energy slip away and didn't feel quite right. I assumed I had picked up a parasite or something from my years of travel to places where I had been in contact with numerous sick people. I wondered if I had TB. My kitchen was filled with laughter as friends and family gathered to celebrate Christmas. I answered the phone in good spirits and was shocked to hear my doctor say she was concerned about my elevated PSA levels indicating the possibility of prostate cancer. I needed to come in for further tests. Numb, I hung up the phone. *Cancer? Me? Impossible. It can't be. There must be a mistake. What if it's true?* I looked at Sarah, the love of my life. I could not speak as I felt those tears in my throat. Would I survive? Was I going to die?

I thought of my kids. I have dreamed of the day I would walk my oldest daughter Natalie down the aisle for her wedding. Would I be here when she received her Ph.D. in child psychology? I wanted to be there for my three red-headed boys Stephan, Nick, and Grant. I held aspirations for their following in my footsteps and living out their lives helping kids all over the world. I had prayed they would do things of greater influence than I had ever dreamed. I heard the squeal of Sophia, my two-year old. I had to be here to watch her grow up!

This can't be happening! I don't have time for this! I'm too busy! So much is going on right now. Hope4Kids is making an amazing impact on the lives of AIDS orphans in Uganda! We are building a hospital!

What about my sponsored teenage Ugandan girls, Sophia and Beatrice? I have been providing for them since they watched their parents die of AIDS. Recently they said they were praying I would live long enough for me to see them get their education and come and work in our Ugandan hospital. I laughed and reminded them I was only fifty-three years old and had decades left! Now I may have cancer. Will I live to see these precious girls fulfill their dreams?

Fighting tears, I finally pulled Sarah aside and told her what my doctor had just said. She reassured me that it probably wasn't cancer, and if it were we would beat it. She would become a source of strength to me over the next months.

Staring across the Maryland countryside, my breathing slowed and I remembered our urologist suggesting we bring a notebook and a pen to write down our questions and his suggestions for treatment. Further tests and biopsies revealed aggressive cancer in the prostate. He was right. I sat dazedly not hearing. I came to when Sarah grabbed my hand. Tears were flowing down her cheeks. Our greatest fears were now giving in to the truth. I had cancer.

Daily, my thoughts and fears would swing like a pendulum. What treatment is available? What are the chances for a cure? Survival? Life expectancy? Has it spread? What about that x-ray that shows spots on the pelvis and neck? What if it is in the lymph nodes?

We knew we needed prayer support. Would God hear our desperate prayers? Sarah sent a heartfelt email to our circle of friends announcing I had cancer and begged for prayer. The support we received was incredible. Friends offered to help in any way they could. Emails filled the inbox on my computer. My African friends were declaring twenty-one days of fasting and prayer. AIDS orphans were praying and fasting for me. My Ugandan daughters were weeping and praying each morning at 5:30 A.M. that their daddy would recover! Cuban friends were praying! Russian and Romanian friends told us they were holding special prayer times. Calls and emails came from all over the world. I spoke to the grade school kids at Joy Christian School in Glendale thanking them for raising money for our orphan program in Peru. When Pastor Paul Sorenson came to the front of the chapel to close in prayer, he surprised me by saying the students were aware that I had cancer and were praying. He presented me with a box of hand-written cards, and the students surrounded me to pray. Those tears packed my throat and splashed down my face as they prayed. I whispered, "God, you must hear the prayers of these kids who shouldn't be burdened with concern for me."

I could hardly wait to read those cards when I returned to my office. Here are a few of my favorites:

"I'm sure you're fighting this disease with all your power. And even if you don't make it, we'll all remember what a wonderful guy you really are."

"Thank you for everything you have done in the past. Your legend will always live on! If you somehow go to Heaven, I can't wait to see you!"

"I wonder how old you are."

Others were a little more encouraging.

"You are very generous. My teacher is your number one fan and I am to. You are are classes hearow. We love you so much. You are very special and you have a kind hert to give all of that to the pour … We all want to see you and we whant you to get will."

"Thanks for everything you do! God provides for even the smallest ant, he gives it life and supply! You've given your life to God to use you, for helping others he will provide for you and help you through this. You just have to keep believing. I know how you feel. My grandma has cancer but God has helped her recover. Have a great day and never stop smiling!"

"I know you can do it! Just like the blind man in the Bible, God will heal you. Don't worry. God will help you!"

"He will not let your foot slip—he who watches over you will not slumber."

"I'm sorry that you have to go through what you are. My aunt has had 4 different cancers, now she has another one! If you have to go to the hospital here's a word of advice, always ask what there doing."

I began reading everything I could find on cancer on the Internet. I learned that a positive attitude was everything! Sarah began cooking organically and insisted I take supplements. Most days I was positive that God was answering the prayers of the many people who had surrounded us. Other times I would have a sense of alarm, depression, and hopelessness. The side effects of the weeks of radiation would exhaust me of the usual energy. A sense of uselessness filled me when I realized I would miss leading a team to Africa. It would be the first time in thirty-three years that I would not be able to lead one of our mission teams.

I knew I had to fight the fears and negative thoughts that so often accompany people with cancer. With all of the people praying, eating right and a positive attitude, I would win this battle!

Everyday I would see some little thing that would allow me to thank God. Family became more special, friends more valuable. I am more grateful each day for new opportunities. Life is beyond precious.

One day as I sat in the waiting room visiting with other cancer patients in for our daily treatments, I realized God could use me in a special way here too. I began praying that God would use me as an encouragement to the others around me. I conversed with a patient whose treatment for prostate cancer had failed, and cancer had spread throughout his body. His prognosis was bleak. Extremely depressed, he no longer cared about anything. I asked him if he had a hobby. He did. He had a collection of electric trains but no longer messed with them. Later his wife told me that after our conversation she had seen a change in his attitude. The following Monday he came in early to talk to me. "Thanks for your enthusiasm and encouragement. I had a great weekend! I even worked on my favorite hobby. I repaired my electric trains!"

Nadel, one of the radiation therapists, said to me. "We know when you are in the waiting room. The other patients come in so optimistic and hopeful. We know you have been talking to them. They love you!"

So, this is my purpose. God, you can use this cancer to bring hope to others!

I watched the water trickle over the rocks of Tuscarora Creek. A sense of gratitude swept over me. *God, I am grateful that you are faithful. You have strengthened me through this difficult storm. I know you will see me through. Whatever the days ahead hold, I am confident you are with me!*

We have witnessed people in Peru struggling through troubled waters. We visited a barrio that had been built upon a garbage dump. People fashioned bricks of sand mixed with garbage. There was about thirty feet of waste beneath their homes. The toxic materials within the walls and underneath the homes were destroying children either by death or causing them to go from normal, healthy children to severely brain damaged children no longer able to speak or care for themselves. We were told one little girl was playing and laughing one day and the next could not get out of bed. She is completely bedridden and offers no response when family members speak to her.

How do you relocate hundreds of families? How do you teach them about their harmful environment?

Baby Tom was hospitalized with pneumonia and had multiple problems. He had a tumor in his chest, kidney problems and a problem with his brain. He was sixteen months old but was the size of a three-month-old. He also had a tumor in his back, and the part of his brain that makes one swallow was missing so he was fed through a tube. The tube was in his nose instead of his abdomen because with no running water and a great lack of understanding of personal hygiene within his home, there was a larger risk of infection. Baby Tom had no knee caps. He had club feet. We were told that his was such a sad case even his Peruvian doctors cried. How do you tell Baby Tom's parents as they hold him and kiss him and whisper to him that nothing can be done for their baby? Once you see him and know his name, it becomes too personal to turn your back.

The schools in the barrios of Trujillo, Peru had no water or electricity. Most students are grossly malnourished and the schools have no means of feeding them. One school asked our team not to bring soccer balls because the kids are so emaciated they don't have the energy to play.

Eighty-five percent of the kids in the poor barrios are unable to attend school. They are left to their own devices and have to find ways to make money for their family. An alarming number of girls become prostitutes at a very young age. Forty percent of the girls become pregnant between the ages of eleven to fourteen!

The vast majority of these kids are abused and raped by their parents, uncles, neighbors and brothers. The stats are shocking and one can not help but wonder where God is in all of this.

We know we have to step up and do something once we see the needs. In each of the six barrios in Peru, we have built community centers where kids come everyday for breakfast and lunch. The centers are run by missionary couples who use the center to educate people on hygiene, family matters, job skills and more. There are now free clinics in each barrio.

Pastor Ruth introduced us to the Karamojong tribe. They are a despised group and treated much like the gypsies are treated in Europe. The kids who have taken to the streets are many and have turned to sniffing glue to make life bearable.

The men sit around pots of home-brewed alcohol and drink from long straws. As their saliva returns to the pot they spread disease to one another, TB being a common one. When they have finished drinking, there is a nasty residue left in the pot which the starving children will scoop out and eat. They become drunk and stumble through the streets cutting themselves on broken bottles and other sharp objects lying in their paths.

The children dig in the trash and beg for food. They are often beaten as they try to steal a donut to silence their growling stomachs. One 10-year-old girl, Maria, found a piece of meat in the trash heap. Someone had put poison on it to kill rats and in fact a dead rat was attached to the meat. She hungrily grabbed the meat and pulled it from the dead rat's mouth. Other children poking in the trash heap spotted her with the meat and ran to take it from her. Quickly she shoved the meat into her mouth. Within hours she became violently ill and died.

When Pastor Ruth brought these children to Rachel's attention, Rachel told her, "We have to do something."

"Yes."

Generous people in the States donated money for large cooking pots, salary for widows to cook the meals and money for food. Ruth said the day they began feeding these children they were suspicious and expected soldiers to be there with trucks to round them up and take them back to Karamoja. First the children were served porridge in cups. Ruth wrote:

"The children kept shouting 'Jesus' with their cups lifted high. They gave the thumbs up sign which shows that Jesus is a hero. They learned this during political campaigns where people praise their candidates. For these children, they realized that Jesus is their candidate and their hero. Tears of joy rolled down my cheeks as I saw the face of Jesus smiling, seeing the little children cheer Him."

The children are bathed with medicated soap and dressed in clean clothes. Many are treated for scabies and worms. Volunteers are teaching them to read and write, as well as manners, so they will be rehabilitated and eventually go to school. Because of their lives on the streets they have not learned to be socially appropriate but are willing to learn.

They are fed a meal in the afternoon of beans and rice and sometimes they get meat. Ruth says, "They think it's Christmas!"

Their parents stand outside the fence and watch as the children eat good, clean food and enjoy a structured day of bathing and learning. They have aspirations for their children as well as for themselves—the women are learning crafts so they can sell their wares and support their families. The entire Karamojong community is becoming a society of dignity and pride.

Although we are far from understanding the difficulties life throws at us, we are so blessed to count on Christ to see us through. Even when we think what we have been dealt stinks, we have the knowledge that God sees us, loves us and has the final say. In our darkest hour we have hope.

Chapter Seven

Another Storm Brews

There is another storm that has been churning since the world began. Most of us are not aware of it even though as Christians we were rescued from it. We have forgotten about the drowning, lost souls surrounding us. We get so involved in our lives, jobs and families we lose sight of our neighbors, friends and relatives who are dying without Christ. Over 120 years ago, William Booth had a vision of these lost souls.

I saw a dark and stormy ocean. Over it the black clouds hung heavily, through which thunder rolled; and every now and then vivid lightning flashed. The winds moaned, and the waves rose and foamed and fretted and broke, and rose to foam and fret and break again.

In that ocean I saw myriads of poor human beings plunging and floating, shrieking and cursing, and struggling and drowning, and as they cursed and shrieked, they rose and shrieked again, then sank to rise no more.

Out of this dark angry ocean I saw a mighty rock rise up above the black clouds that overhung the stormy sea. Around the base of this rock I saw a vast platform and up on to this platform I saw with delight a number of the poor, struggling, drowning wretches continually climbing out of the angry ocean.

As I looked more closely, I found a number of those who had been rescued scheming and contriving by ladders and ropes and boats to deliver the poor strugglers out of this sea. Here and there were some who actually jumped in regardless of all consequences in their eagerness to save the poor drowning multitudes. I hardly know which gladdened me most, the sight of the poor creatures who climbed the rocks and reached the place of safety, or the devotion and self-sacrifice of those whose sole purpose was to rescue others from the sea.

As I looked I saw that the occupants of the platform were quite a mixed company. They were divided into different sets or classes and they occupied themselves in quite different ways. It was only a very few, comparatively, who seemed to make it their business to get the people out of the sea.

What puzzled me most was that though all had been rescued at one time or another from the ocean, nearly everyone seemed to have forgotten all about it. The memory of its darkness and danger no longer troubled them; and what was equally strange and perplexing to me was that these people did not seem to have any care—that is, any agonizing care—about the poor perishing ones who were struggling and drowning right in front of them; many of whom were their own husbands and wives and mothers and sisters and children.

This lack of concern could not have been because they were ignorant of what was going on. They lived right in sight of it all. They talked about it sometimes and regularly went to hear lectures, which described the awful state of things.

I have already said that the occupants of this platform were engaged in different pursuits. Some were absorbed night and day in trading in order to make gain, storing up their savings in boxes and by other means. Many passed their time amusing themselves with growing flowers on the side of the rock; others by painting pieces of cloth, perfoming music, or by dressing themselves up in different ways and walking about to be admired. Some occupied themselves with eating and drinking. Others were greatly taken up with arguing about the poor drowning creatures in the sea and what would become of them, while many appeased their conscience by participating in round after round of curious religious ceremonies.

As I looked more closely I saw that some had found a passage up the rock leading to a higher platform, far above the black clouds that overhung the ocean. From this elevated platform, they had a good view of the mainland, which was not very far away, and to which they expected to be taken off at some distant day. Here they passed their time in pleasant thoughts, congratulating themselves and each other on being rescued from the stormy deep, and singing songs about the happiness they were to enjoy when they should be taken to the mainland.

All this time the struggling, shrieking multitudes were floating about in the dark sea, quite near by, close enough to be pulled to safety. Instead, however they continued to perish in full view of those on the rock, not only one by one, but sinking down in the shoals, sinking down every day in the dark and angry sea.

As I looked, I found that the handful whom I had observed before were still toiling in their rescue work. Oh, how I wished there had been a multitude of them! Indeed they did little else but fret and cry and toil and scheme for the perishing people. They gave themselves no rest, and bothered everyone around them to come and help with the rescue work. In fact, they came to be voted a real nuisance by many quite benevolent and kindhearted people, and many who were very religious too. But still they went on, spending all they had and all they could get, on boats and rafts and drags and ropes, and every other imaginable thing they could invent for saving the poor, wretched, drowning people.

There were a few others who did much the same thing at times, working hard in their own way, but the people who attracted my attention were those who were totally committed to the task. They went at it with such fierceness and fury that many, including those who were doing the same kind of work in a milder way, called them mad.

And then I saw something more wonderful still. The miseries and agonies and perils and blasphemies of the poor struggling people in this dark sea moved the pity of the great God in Heaven, so much so that He sent a Great Being to deliver them. This Great Being whom Jehovah sent came straight from His palace, right through the black clouds, and leapt into the raging sea among the drowning, sinking people. As I watched I saw Him toiling to rescue them, with tears and cries, until the sweat of His great anguish ran down in blood.

As He toiled and embraced the poor wretches and tried to lift them on to the rock, He cried out continually to those already rescued—to those whom He had helped up with His own bleeding hands—to come and help Him in the painful and laborious task of saving others from the sea.

What seemed to me to be so strange was that those on the platform to whom He called—who heard His voice and felt they ought to obey it, at least they said they did—those who loved Him much, and were in full sympathy with Him in the task He had undertaken—who worshipped Him—or professed to do so, did not respond. They were so taken up with their trades and professions and money saving and pleasures and families and circles and religion and arguments about it and the preparation for going to the mainland, that they did not attend to the cry that came to them from Him out of the ocean. If they heard it they did not heed it. They did not care and so the multitude went on struggling and shrieking and drowning in darkness and anguish.

Another Storm Brews
///

And then I saw something that seemed to me the strangest of all that I had seen in this strange vision. I saw that some of these people on the platform whom this wonderful Being wanted to come and help Him, heedless of His cries to them, were always praying and crying for Him to come to them. They wanted Him to come and stay with them, to spend His time and strength on them.

Firstly, they wanted Him to make them happier. Secondly, they wanted Him to take away the doubts and misgivings they had respecting the truth of some letters which this great Being had written them. Then, they wanted Him to make them feel more secure on the rock—so secure that they would be quite sure they should never slip off again. Finally, they wanted Him to make them feel quite certain that they would really reach the mainland some day, because it was well-known that some had walked so carelessly as to miss their footing, and had fallen back into the stormy waters.

These people used to meet and get as high up the rock as they could, then, looking towards the mainland where they thought the Great Being was, they would cry out, "Come to us! Come and help us!" And all this time he was down among the poor, struggling, drowning creatures in the angry deep, with His arms around them, trying to drag them out, and looking up—oh, so longingly, but all in vain, to those on the rock, crying to them, with His voice all hoarse and calling, "Come to Me! Come and help Me!" …

My comrades, you are rescued from the waters—you are on the rock. He is in the dark sea, calling on you to come to Him and help Him. Will you go?

Look for yourselves. The surging sea of perishing souls rolls up to the very spot on which you stand. This is no vision or imagination I speak of now. It is as real as the Bible; as real as the Christ who hung upon the Cross; as real as the Judgment Day will be;

and as real as the Heaven and hell that will follow it.

Look! Don't be deluded by appearances—men and things are not what they seem. My vision was merely a picture, but the reality is far more harrowing than any vision or picture can possibly be. All who are not on the rock are in the sea. Look at them from the standpoint of the Great White Throne and what a sight you have. Jesus Christ, the Son of God, is in the midst of this dying multitude, working to save them. And He is calling on you to jump into the sea, to go right away to His side and help Him.

Will you jump? Will you go to His feet and place yourself absolutely at His disposal? As when a man on a river-bank sees another struggling in the water, lays aside the outer garments that would hinder his efforts and jumps in to the rescue, so will you who still linger on the bank thinking and singing and praying about the poor struggling souls lay aside your shame, your pride, your care about other people's opinions, your love of ease and all other selfish love that have hindered you for so long, and jump to the rescue of this multitude of dying souls?

Does the surging sea look dark and dangerous? Perhaps so. There is no doubt that the leap, for you as for every one who takes it, means distress, scorn, and suffering. For you it may mean more than this. It may mean death. He who calls to you from the sea, however, knows what it will mean; and knowing it, he still beckons you and bids you come.

You must do it. You cannot hold back. You have enjoyed yourself in religion long enough. You have sung. You have had pleasant feelings, pleasant songs, pleasant meetings, and pleasant prospects. There has been much human happiness, much clapping of hands, very much of Heaven on earth.

Now, then, go to God and tell him you are prepared to turn your back upon it all, and that you are willing to spend the rest of your days grappling with these perishing multitudes.

You must do it. You must go down amongst the perishing

crowds. Your happiness now consists in sharing their misery, your ease in sharing their pain, your crown in bearing their cross, and your Heaven in going to the very jaws of hell to rescue them. Will you answer His call? Will you go?[9]

I want to be among the rescuers. I do not want to just go to church and thank God for saving me. There is an urgency to go into the world. We need to grab onto our kids, parents, cousins, family and friends and pull them from the stormy sea before they are lost for eternity. We need to answer the call and pray that others will hear Him calling. "Jesus went through all the towns and villages, teaching in their synagogues, preaching the good news of the kingdom and healing every disease and sickness. When he saw the crowds, he had compassion on them, because they were harassed and helpless, like sheep without a shepherd. Then he said to his disciples, "The harvest is plentiful but the workers are few. Ask the Lord of the harvest, therefore, to send out workers into his harvest field"(Matthew 9:35-38).

What kind of Christian is being developed in the average American church? I see a trend that troubles me. It is one of self-centeredness, inward looking and growing fearful of this world which has many Christians retreating behind the safety of the church walls. This produces a religious attitude of prejudice toward those who are not within those walls.

While many alarming things are happening we cannot retreat in fear. Societies are collapsing because of moral decay and lawlessness which has resulted in suffering beyond description. I witnessed this in graphic detail while in Haiti one Easter season. Haiti is the poorest nation in this hemisphere. The collapse of the infrastructure is shocking. In Puerto Prince, the capital city, the roads were mostly impassable, water was scarcely available and the city was without electrical power with the exception of a few hours in the middle of the night. It was as if Satan himself was destroying lives through destitution, sickness and poverty.

One night I felt the power of Satan like I rarely have in my life. A voodoo band consisting of several hundred people was on the streets outside my hotel. One person was painted red representing Satan. The crowd was celebrating that Jesus was dead and proclaiming that He had not risen from the grave. They were beating on drums, blowing whistles, chanting, casting curses on people, screaming and drinking themselves senseless. The power of evil was so strong I began praying in the spirit and proclaiming the blood of Jesus. The Scripture says:

> Be self-controlled and alert. Your enemy the devil prowls around like a roaring lion looking for someone to devour. Resist him, standing firm in the faith, because you know that your brothers throughout the world are undergoing the same kind of sufferings. (1 Peter 5:8-9)

James 4:7 says, "Submit yourselves, then, to God. **Resist** the devil, and he will **flee** from you" (Author's emphasis).

The following morning two women on their way to our church service found a drunken man passed out along the road. They tried to waken him by splashing water on his face. He remained motionless so they placed their hands on him and prayed for him to become sober and awake. Immediately he stood up, sober. They brought him to church, and as they entered I was talking about a time I was speaking in Russia and drunken men were made sober by the power of Christ. The ladies were so struck by the timing they began to cry and called for the pastor to come outside. He prayed with the man to receive Christ. That evening the man returned with his wife and three children. He stood up and gave a testimony to the power of Christ and told how he had now been saved.

Once while in Uganda Rachel met a man who experienced a turbulent storm. Just outside the entrance of the church, she was visiting a young man; Michael broke into her thoughts. "Sister Rachel, I want you to meet Issa. He is a new brother in Christ. He was a Muslim and just yesterday has decided to follow Jesus." She whirled around. She had heard snatches of his amazing conversion.

She extended her hand. "Issa. I'm so glad to meet you." Pulling a chair across from him she sat down and leaned toward him. "Issa. Will you tell me your story?"

I was raised as a Muslim. It's all I've ever known. I was a devoted Muslim and at no time had I ever imagined becoming a Christian. Above all I despised Christians as high class infidels. I wanted everyone to be a Muslim. I've studied in Kenya and traveled with six of my Moslim brothers to a mosque in Mbale. Our purpose was to fast and pray and to recruit others to our faith during Ramadan.

One night I dreamed of being in a pit with the rest of the group from Kenya, and a large crowd was also in the pit wailing and crying for help. The pit was very big and deep. While everybody was struggling for help, I discovered a ladder just by my side. I then decided to use it. As I climbed the ladder, I wondered where is this ladder leading? I looked up into the clouds and discovered the ladder was being held in place by a cross. I stopped because Muslims don't like the cross. I knew I couldn't go near it. I tried to back down the ladder but someone was behind me. I couldn't go back and I couldn't go up. I was so afraid I forced myself to wake up from this dream. My heart was pounding loudly. I was afraid to go back to sleep. I finally nodded off and the dream picked up exactly where it had left off. I found myself halfway up the ladder to the cross with no way of backing down. Again, trembling and sweating, I forced myself to waken and remained awake and terrified the remainder of the night.

The following night I dreamed this same dream. This time I heard a voice calling my name and saying, 'If only you can come out of this pit by using the cross you will not only save yourself but you will also save the rest of those who are in the pit by showing them the way out.'

The next night I had another dream. I was in a crowd of people. There was chaos everywhere. Fear was in the air. I sensed a real danger with no way of escape. Suddenly someone called out, 'This way!' Relieved, I ran toward the opening. Upon reaching it I realized it was the door to a church. You could run through the front door, past the altar and out the back door to safety. I could not go near the cross on the altar. Sweating in fear, I willed myself to wake up from my dream. I sat up and tried to stay awake. I drifted off again with the dream taking off in the same spot it had left off. I shook off sleep and woke my Muslim brothers. I told them about the dreams. They told me perhaps a Christian has bewitched me and I should forget about it. They read from the Koran to chase away these ideas and began cursing all forms of witchcraft that might have been done against me by some Christian.

That night I tried not to sleep but sleep overtook me. Again I dreamed of a ladder leading out of a pit. This time I looked to the top of a ladder and saw a bright light. Words appeared written in blood. At this time I was wide awake. The light and the words remained. A voice told me to write down the words. I grabbed a pen and paper and began to write the words which were in Arabic. I called my friends together and told them about this last vision. They were excited. Maybe Muhammad had sent a message to me. Together we began to interpret the message. It read, 'I am the true God, Jesus…' When my brothers read those words they demanded that I stop. They believed I was demon possessed. They left me alone and said I had better read the Koran.

In the morning we were preparing for prayers. As you know, Muslims have to wash their feet, hands and head before they pray. I turned on the water and blood came from the faucet. I jumped back and told my brothers, 'You know we cannot touch blood before prayers.' They pushed me aside and turned on the water. While I was seeing blood, they were seeing clear water. They came to the conclusion that I had gone mad and left me alone. I was then struck by a very bright light and I heard a voice calling me: 'The blood that you see was shed on your behalf. Now come out of where you are and go join the true worshipers. Worship me in Truth and Spirit, for I have chosen you this day to bring you out of death into life and have appointed you to bring my people out of darkness into my everlasting light. Now do as I say.' Then the light vanished. I called my friends in and told them about it. Convinced I had gone completely mad, they decided to beat me. Maybe they could beat it out of me before it was too late. When they realized it wasn't working they discussed tying me up and taking me to a mental institution. Then they said I was an infidel who deserved to die. I fought back and ran out of the mosque.

A man was standing outside with a Bible. He asked me if I wanted to know the way to the cross. I said, "Yes. But right now they are chasing me." The man quickly hired two bicycle taxis and we escaped. He took me to his home. I had only my white robe. He gave me this suit of clothes I am wearing and told me there were churches in Tororo who helped Muslims who wanted to become Christians. I said I would like to go there, so he paid for my passage. My documents, money and clothes were all at the mosque, but I didn't dare go back to get them.

When I arrived in Tororo I asked around and was sent to True Vine Ministries. Here I found someone to lead me to Christ. I have been waiting to see what I should do next. I have received messages on my cell phone that I need to pick up my documents and return to Kenya. Our leaders there said since one of us has gone mad, we all need to return so as to not embarrass them. I have spoken to my wife. She said they have already contacted her and told her she should divorce me because I have gone mad."

Intrigued, Rachel leaned in. "Is she in danger? Are you in danger?"

Issa nodded. "Three years ago my twin brother became a Christian. They forced his wife to drink poison and killed her. They also tried to kill my brother. He had to go into hiding."

Shifting in her chair, Rachel asked, "What is your next move?"

"Well, I have been seeking counsel here at True Vine. I need to get my documents. I want to go for my wife and little girl. I hope they will come with me and I will bring them back here."

"Is it safe for you to go get them?"

"It may be because they don't yet know that I have chosen to be a Christian. So far they just think I've gone mad."

Issa spent the next couple of days around the church. Men continued to counsel him in his new faith. He was anxious to go home to his wife, so Michael took him to retrieve his documents from the police station and paid his passage back to Kenya. For the next two weeks Rachel asked daily, "Has anyone heard from Issa?" They had not.

About four months later Rachel received an email from Issa.

Praise the Lord I am fine and blessed of the Lord. I am just writing to pass a word of greeting to you and to break the long silence after the last time we met at Uganda True Vine Tabernacle. I am Issa the Muslim who got born again miraculously in Uganda last year. I have undergone many challenges in life, but the Lord has seen me through victoriously. In fact I have joined my brother's evangelistic ministry which targets Muslims worldwide known as Muslims for Christ World Evangelism. I am joining a Bible college on the third week of March. Sincerely speaking ever since my conversion to Christianity, I have nothing to regret about my new life even though my wife divorced me, and my properties were set ablaze, and my dad also disowned me, but surely the Lord has seen me through all this. Please stand with me in your prayers as I commit my studies to the Lord to enable me to obtain the fees for them. As for now I have nothing to live for but the Lord.

Rachel and Issa correspond through email, and when Rachel returned to Uganda Issa traveled two hours to see her. He was happy and well. He and his brother are doing important work and have started an orphanage for children of converted Muslims who have been killed for accepting Christ. They have a tremendous outreach to Muslims and provide solid Christian training for those who turn to Jesus.

"If you want to be my disciple, you must hate everyone else by comparison—your father and mother, wife and children, brothers and sisters—yes, even your own life. Otherwise, you cannot be my disciple. And if you do not carry your own cross and follow me, you cannot be my disciple. But don't begin until you count the cost. For who would begin construction of a building without first calculating the cost to see if there is enough money to finish it?" (Luke 14:26-28) (NLT).

We live in a wicked world where Satan's attacks are visible. If we are going to make a difference, we are going to have to proclaim the risen Christ in all His power. This is not the time to retreat. It is a time to advance the Kingdom of God. It is going to take a compassionate church to see beyond its own needs. It will take Christians who deeply care for people in need and are willing to sacrifice and take risks for the cause of Christ. To truly become more like Jesus is not to become more religious but to love the people of this world and to be concerned for their souls. In order to reach the world we need to live a life of worship.

Chapter Eight

Living a Life of Worship

I have experienced various styles of worship throughout the world. The Russian Orthodox Church leaves me in awe of God's holy presence. Their services are solemn with candles, icons, incense and confession. There is ritual and celebration. When the gospel is read, the lights go up and the music volume rises. The buildings and land are strikingly beautiful. I have been told the Orthodox believe the house of God should be the most elaborate of all buildings and prefer their churches to be on a hill or near water, representing a jewel. They say the place where you pray should almost have an enchanting atmosphere to represent standing in the Holy Presence of our Lord.

When the Romanian Pentecostals, African Methodists, or Cuban believers worship with shouts of praise and dance, it makes me wish I had rhythm. Taking part in the quiet humility of worship in a house church in China or Vietnam subdues my spirit. Primarily we consider worship to be those times we draw away from the world and deliberately focus on God through our singing, praising and praying. This is important but it doesn't end there. We must live out a life of worship.

We don't have any record of Jesus singing in the Temple, but didn't

His life reflect glorifying the Father in all that he did? Every time He touched someone whether it was a healing, feeding the 5,000 or dying on the cross, He was honoring the Heavenly Father and bringing glory to Him in His deeds of worship.

We worship God by the way we respond to the needs in our community, school, place of work, neighborhood, country and our world. "Therefore, I urge you, brothers, in view of God's mercy, to offer your bodies as living sacrifices, holy and pleasing to God—this is your *spiritual act of worship* (Romans 12:1 Author's emphasis).

I love how the Message Bible puts it:

"So here's what I want you to do, God helping you: Take your everyday, ordinary life—your sleeping, eating, going-to-work, and walking-around life—and place it before God as an offering. Embracing what God does for you is the best thing you can do for him." (Romans 12:1 Message)

Mother Teresa went to the poorest of poor in Calcutta, living with them and serving as Christ served. She said:

Each time anyone comes into contact with us, they must become different and better people because of having met us. We must radiate God's love. We must know that we have been created for greater things. Not just for diplomas and degrees, not just be a number in the world, this work or that work. We have been created in order to *love* and *be loved.* Love does not measure…it just gives.

Over thirty years ago I was a co-speaker at a conference with Corrie Ten Boom, author of *The Hiding Place* (2006).x In our few moments alone, she reminded me, "God never allows anyone to cross our path that He does not intend to use us in their lives or use them in ours."

While leading a team in Romania, I spoke on living an existence of divine service. I read:

I was hungry and you fed me,

I was thirsty and you gave me a drink,

I was homeless and you gave me a room,

I was shivering and you gave me clothes,

I was sick and you stopped to visit,

I was in prison and you came to me . . .

I'm telling the solemn truth: Whenever you did one of these things to someone overlooked or ignored, that was me—you did it to me. (Matthew 25:35-40 Message)

I challenged the team; "Today when someone comes across your path, know that Jesus sent them. In fact, the very first person you meet, I want you to think of that person as Jesus. Do what you need to do for him and then whisper, 'As unto You, Jesus.'" We began our day in anticipation of who Jesus would have us unexpectedly meet.

There are many gypsy, bandit street kids in Romania. The first person I met was one of those street kids. A boy of about twelve years came alongside my interpreter and me as we walked. I kept walking. The boy stayed with us and continued speaking to my interpreter. *This can't be who Jesus wants me to serve today. He's probably begging for something.* I continued walking but the boy was persistent. Finally, out of irritation, I asked my interpreter, "What does he want?"

"He's saying that he lives under a bridge and takes care of other children. They are hungry, and he wants to know if you can just buy them a little bread and pasta."

"Show me the bridge."

We found young children huddled together under the bridge. I couldn't could not buy food fast enough. I almost missed Jesus because of my attitude. Through tears of humility, I whispered, "As unto You, Jesus," and presented the children with pasta, oil and bread.

It is so easy in our hurried lives to pass by those God puts in front of us. One day Rachel and her granddaughter Jordan were sitting outside Cold Stone Creamery enjoying ice cream after seeing a movie. They watched a mother walking around with her nine-year-old daughter. She approached people and spoke to them. The people would shake their heads or totally ignore her and walk away. When Rachel and Jordan stood to throw away their left-over ice cream, the woman approached them. She was holding tightly to the hand of her beautiful, shy daughter. She said, "I need money for a few groceries for my children."

Rachel told her. "I'm sorry. I have no cash," Then walked a few steps and turned back. "Do you live near here?"

"Yes. We are living with my aunt."

"Do you have a car?"

"It's my aunt's car."

Rachel took Jordan by the hand and walked away toward her car. She divulged to Jordan: "I do have my debit card. We could take them to the Super Wal-Mart next door and buy her some food. But…well…she lives with her aunt. So, it's not like they are really desperate…."

Jordan couldn't believe her grandma who travels all the way to Africa to help children would walk away from that woman and child. "Dee Dee," she argued. "You have your debit card. We could go get groceries."

"Okay. Let's pray and see if God *really* wants us to help them." She uttered a quick prayer, started the car and drove to the area where the mother and child were begging. "Okay," she told Jordan, "if they are still in sight then we'll buy them groceries."

They were. Rachel drove up and said to the woman, "I don't have any cash, but if you meet me in front of Wal-Mart, I can buy you some groceries with my debit card." *I'm sure she will turn me down because a lot of people who beg really don't want food. They just want money.*

The lady smiled, "Okay."

As the four of them went through the grocery department, they introduced themselves. The woman's name was Terri and her daughter was Irene. Irene was shy and didn't say anything but smiled whenever Rachel said anything to her. Terri said she had two other children and had come to Arizona with her husband but didn't know he had a girlfriend here. He abandoned the family, leaving them with Terri's aunt while he went to live with his girlfriend. Terri couldn't read nor write and had no skills to offer in the workplace.

When the shopping was finished the little group stood outside of Wal-Mart. Rachel leaned down to Irene and touched her arm. "Do you know why we did this today?" Irene shook her head. "We did it because we want you to know Jesus loves you very much. Do not ever forget that. Jesus loves you."

One of Rachel's heroes is Pastor Jim from Michigan. He rides a Harley motorcycle, loves people and is a tremendous example of living a life of worship.

One day Pastor Jim rolled into the gas station on his Harley and spotted a tough- looking biker filling his Harley. When he stood in line to pay, he noticed the biker standing a few people behind him. Jim told the cashier his pump number and added, "I want to pay for his gas too."

The cashier called to the biker, "What pump are you on?"

"What 'cha wanna' know that for?"

"This guy wants to pay for your gas."

The tough guy stared at the squeaky clean, grinning young man standing with his open wallet. "What 'cha wanna' do that for?"

"Oh. I thought God would just like to bless you today."

"Hey. You must be that preacher I heard about." The biker relaxed and shook Pastor Jim's hand. "A lot of my biker friends say that you're their preacher."

Pastor Jim hasn't always sought out bikers but that was before he had met Rat. Mark, a friend of Pastor Jim's, approached him and said he had a buddy who was dying of cancer and would Pastor Jim go see him. On the ride over Mark said, "By the way, this guy we're seeing. He hates pastors."

"What! Why does he hate pastors?"

"Because he called a pastor in the area and told him he was dying and he had a couple questions. When he asked the pastor to come to see him, the pastor told him he only visits members of his church."

As they drove a little further Mark said, "Oh, and he's a biker. His name is Rat."

So Pastor Jim walked up to Rat's trailer, knocked on the door and walked in. Rat was sitting on the sofa. He was covered with tattoos and had long hair, but only a few strands remained as the result of chemo treatments. Rat looked at Pastor Jim and demanded, "Who the _____ are you?"

"Well, before I answer that, I just want to say one thing. Remember that pastor you called and he wouldn't come out to see you? Well, he's a jerk!"

"Yah. But who are you?"

"Well, I'm a pastor and I'm here to answer any questions you might have, and I'll stay all afternoon if that is what it takes. But I want to ask you a question first."

"Ask."

"I understand you're dying. When you die are you going to go to heaven?"

Tears spilled over and flowed down the face of the hard-core biker. "When I was eight years old I accepted Jesus as my personal Savior. I know I belong to God but I've been rebellious. I've been a disgrace to my Christianity. I know God's tired of dealing with me. He's tired of the way I've been living so He's taking me home because I'm no good to Him anymore."

Pastor Jim sat across from Rat. "Well, that's all I wanted to know. Now what are your questions for me?"

"I've only got one, Pastor."

"What is that?"

"The club I ride with. When a member dies, they are cremated and the ashes are sprinkled in the gas tanks of all the guys, and they take you for one last ride. Is it okay with God if I get cremated? That's all I wanna' know."

"That body of yours is just a shell anyway. God doesn't really care if you do or don't. That's up to you."

Pastor Jim took Rat's hands in his as they prayed together and became friends.

A few weeks later Rat died and Pastor Jim was asked to conduct his funeral. When he went to see the family, Rat's wife told him that all of Rat's friends were at the Red Devil Restaurant. Pastor Jim had noticed the rows of Harleys there when he drove into town on his own Harley. On the way out of town as he neared the Red Devil, God spoke to him: "Listen, if you're going to love those guys you'd better go meet them."

"God, I really don't want to meet them."

"If you're going to love those guys, you'd better go meet them."

Pastor Jim reluctantly pulled into the restaurant. When he walked in, he said it looked like a scene out of a 1970's Hell's Angels movie. The restaurant was filled with biker men and women. Pastor Jim stood awkwardly as all eyes stared. He raised his hand in a hesitant wave. "Hi. I'm the pastor who's going to be doing Rat's funeral and I thought I'd just come in and say…Hi."

One of the guys hollered, "Whose Harley is that?"

"That's mine."

He slapped Pastor Jim on the back. "Sit down! Have a beer!"

"Well, I don't do the beer thing but I'll sit down."

The next day when Pastor Jim arrived at the funeral on his Harley, all the bikers were there and they had a special spot for him to park his Harley. Many of that crowd still boast today, "That's my pastor. When I die he's gonna' take care of me."

He was asked, "Who do you ride for?"

"Well, I ride for H.I.M."

"What's that stand for?"

"Hogs in Ministry."

That's when Pastor Jim really began his outreach to bikers. He says, "I realized the churches hadn't sought out bikers; they weren't loving the whole world that Jesus died for. We pick and choose who we're going to love and accept in our churches by the way they dress and look."

Every year Faith Baptist Church in Waterford, Michigan hosts Biker Sunday. Hundreds and hundreds of bikers show up. In fact, the event has gotten so popular they can no longer hold it at the church but at a local fairground. Individual lives and families are transformed through this outreach.

My friend, Leo, knows what it is to meet Jesus in the trenches. He befriends those who are cast aside by society. Wherever he goes he looks for the downtrodden. In his small town in Iowa, he has a reputation for buying groceries and gas, and paying rent and utilities for those who are going through tough times. He takes every opportunity to point those he helps to the cross of Jesus.

While on vacation in Los Angeles, he met a homeless man living under a bridge. Every morning Leo took coffee and donuts to his new friend, and while they shared breakfast Leo told him, "Jesus loves you."

Leo picks up hitchhikers, stops to help people in stalled vehicles and has even paid to have a couple's car towed 125 miles to their home! Now Leo is battling esophageal cancer and everyone around him is asking, "Why Leo? Why does someone who does absolutely nothing to help a person along life's road live to be 100 and someone like Leo who is constantly in the throes of life's struggles pulling people to safety gets knocked down like that?"

I have seen a hug bring a young boy to Christ when I was in South Africa speaking at a series of tent meetings. Each night many curious people crowded inside the tent, and one night as I began preaching a ragged, dirty boy about nine years old walked in and sat down in the second row.

Instantly I felt great concern and compassion for him. He immediately fell asleep and slept through my entire sermon.

Afterward I was greeting people at the back of the tent, and as he approached I reached out for him, but he ran away frightened. I was told he was one of the hundreds of beggar children in this village whose families were unable to care for their children, so they live on the streets and find whatever they can to eat in the garbage.

Sleep did not come easy that night. I kept thinking about that little guy and prayed that God would direct him back to the meeting. He returned the next night and again slept through the service. I waited for him at the back of the tent and this time I blocked the opening and grabbed him in a hug. He was trembling. All of a sudden his little arms went around my back. He must have locked his hands together to get such a tight grip on me. His trembling stopped. No longer afraid, he just held on.

I told him he could sleep in the tent where he would be safe. The next night he was wide awake for the message, and when I asked people to come to the altar to accept Christ, he slipped from his seat and joined the others at the front. Together we wept and hugged at the altar as he asked Jesus to be Lord of his life. I truly believe that hug brought this little guy into the kingdom.

Pastor Ruth, a visionary and a tower of strength in the middle of a poverty stricken neighborhood in Tororo, Uganda knows how to worship with her life. She is not afraid to ask people to meet the needs of the suffering and will go to parliament members, the mayor, shopkeepers, and even the Americans if she thinks they will help her in her cause. While in Tororo I had the honor of meeting with her several times. Each time I was more impressed as I saw her heart for the hurting and watched her take action to feed the street children, train women, care for widows, serve people infected with AIDS, and more as she determines to make a difference in each life.

She goes to the homes of the poorest of poor and recruits people to help fix up homes, fix meals, and counsel people. Desperate people show up at her office and know they will not be turned away as did seventeen-year-old Evelyn who was raped with the result being an unwanted pregnancy. Her attempt at a self-induced abortion caused the baby to be born three months early. The child lived and an angry Evelyn sat across from Ruth wondering why God had permitted this all to happen to her. Ruth, not being immune to heartache, could not explain the whys but shared with her that God did care what happened to her and loved her very much. The baby was three months old and Evelyn had not bothered to give him a name. When Ruth asked if she could name the baby, Evelyn disinterestedly agreed. Ruth and her friend Patsy chose to call him Samuel.

Ruth decided to go to Evelyn's home to see what the family's needs were. Neighbors stopped her and asked where she thought she was going. When she told them, they informed her that the father of that girl was a thief and had been beaten to death when they caught him stealing. Now his wife and all the children were thieves. The neighbors continued with tales of all the bad acts this family had committed and expressed shock that an upstanding woman of the community would bother with the likes of them. Ruth answered: "That is why they need to be loved. Even me. I was nothing good. I was a very bitter woman. I was rejected. So I know. Jesus changed my life. This family can change. What is impossible for men is possible for God." She strode past the protesting neighbors and entered the family's home.

Ruth later told Rachel: "Sister Rachel. When I looked at the poverty of those people, I sat quietly and repented in my heart. *God forgive me for asking for more. You have already given me more than I deserve.* Sometimes we go on our knees and ask Him for more. When we look at these people, we know God himself cares for them and as we reach out to show love to them, we are thankful to God that He will use people like us for such a time as this."

Ruth recruited a team to fix up Evelyn's family's home, people donated blankets and food, and surrounded the family with love. The children no longer steal and their house is becoming one of dignity.

Pastor Ruth has dreams. Slowly she is purchasing land and imagines building a safe haven for who she calls chosen children (street kids and orphans) who face so much condemnation. She longs for a school to teach skills and counseling for AIDS patients. She wants to expand her women's projects to include a supermarket to sell their wares to the surrounding community. She dreams of a guest house and a conference room to rent out for meetings and a restaurant. She wants an internet café....

She visualizes a retreat center for women—for pastor's wives. A place where they can come to be pampered and served; a place away from all of the struggles of home for a few days. Not only will they teach the Word of God but they will teach nutrition and health. She hopes to have chickens, goats and other farm animals so they will have eggs, milk and vegetables from the gardens for feeding the women and other guests who will be on the property.

She tells people: "When I first started out I didn't have anything—only a heart to help the suffering." Pastor Ruth's efforts are endless in her desire to bring hope to the downhearted and to bring people to the knowledge Jesus' love. She constantly dreams of doing more, and God is blessing her tremendously.

Mishu, the pastor to a Romanian gypsy village has eight children and makes very little money. He would work for free and almost does. People come to him, and he will spend out of his own meager income so they can have flour and not go hungry. He had no roof on his house, and last winter his family huddled in one room in order to stay warm. Alina, another missionary to the gypsies, told us he never complains and constantly gives.

We thought this hero should be honored so we told Alina a team member wanted to pay for a roof on Mishu's house. Alina, who has great needs of her own, lit up and you could see the joy on her face and hear it in her voice as she wept: "Oh! I am so happy for him! I can't wait to tell him!" Mishu buried his face in his hands and was unable to speak when she told him the news and again she said, "Nobody deserves it more than Mishu. He sacrifices so much for the people here." Never have I seen such joy for another receiving a gift. Alina and her husband don't have their own home, but her thoughts and delight for Mishu added her to my list of heroes living a life of worship.Putting diapers on babies with AIDS in Russia is an act of worship to your King who gave His life for you. Placing shoes on the feet of a child is worship to your Savior whose feet were pierced for you. Buying food and clothes for the needy is worship to your Lord who watches over you with his compassionate love. Speaking words of tenderness or showing love to an abandoned or hurting child is worship to Him who embraces us with His mercy.

As you strive to live this life of worship that we have all been called to remember the words of Jesus:

I was hungry and you fed me,

I was thirsty and you gave me a drink,

I was homeless and you gave me a room,

I was shivering and you gave me clothes,

I was sick and you stopped to visit,

I was in prison and you came to me… I'm telling you the solemn truth: Whenever you did one of these things to someone overlooked or ignored, that was me—you did it to me." (Matthew 25:34-40 Message)

Chapter Nine

He is Here

by Rachel Eggum Cinader

For thirty-five years Hope4Kids has reached out to orphans and children in need all over the world. James 1:27 says, "Religion that God our Father accepts as pure and faultless is this: to look after orphans and widows in their distress and to keep oneself from being polluted by the world."

Wait! It says orphans *and* widows!

I have been to Uganda nine times in three years. From the very first I met women and heard their stories of despair. The unjust status of women being equal to an animal and their status based on their dowry has concerned me. Husbands often reflect how they bought their wives just as they bought cows and chickens. All are considered property.

Women must deal with co-wives and often exist within the same household. They are subjected to the will of their husband, moving from wife to wife as he pleases.

As I interviewed women, most of whom were widows, I have come to realize the widows of Uganda are in crisis. Husbands are dying of AIDS and are leaving behind multiple wives and children. In this culture of polygamy, women stand by in fear as their co-wives suffer and die of

AIDS—knowing they will be next—praying they won't. They are not only left with their own children to raise but the children of their co-wives. Children are starving at home and take to the streets hoping they will at least find something to eat.

Small children are left to their own devices as their mothers struggle to survive. Some women resort to prostitution. Some widows sell their children for sex for as little as a bar of soap. Some commit suicide. Others wonder if they should poison their children and then themselves… Or would the children be better off if they ran away…. Rejected by family and community, they are convinced God has forgotten them. Some have seen a ray of hope in Pastor Ruth's organization, Smile Africa Ministries.

Pastor Ruth has seen the plight of the widows and orphans and has been doing a great deal to reach out to them. I had heard much about this amazing woman of vision and asked if I could interview her for my book. As I listened to her talk, my love and admiration grew tremendously.

Of the widow Pastor Ruth says, "She is a living, walking-around person but dead on the inside with no hope."

She said, "God will never send someone to you unless He knows there is something He wants you to do in the life of that person." I wondered if she had ever heard of Corrie Ten Boom.

She opened her doors to teach women how to sew on treadle sewing machines. When they graduate, they are allowed to take the sewing machine with them to start their own business, or they can remain at the Smile Africa shop and take part in making uniforms and special orders for Americans and fellow Ugandans. With the pay they receive, they can buy food, pay their rent and live a life of dignity.

Not everyone learns to sew. Some love to cook and are given start-up fees as well as utensils and serving items so they can sell lunches and dinners to those working in town or along the roadside. Others sit inside their dimly lit homes or outside making beads for necklaces and bracelets from strips of paper.

We traveled around hearing widow's stories of desperation and tried to comfort them as they broke down sobbing—many wishing they would die too. We knew we had to partner with Pastor Ruth and reach as many widows and children as possible.

When we set a widow up in business or pay school fees for her children, we are investing in the future. These women and children who were without aspirations now realize that God sees them and now know they have a chance not only to survive, but they can actually have dreams of becoming doctors, nurses, teachers, business owners and more.

Some of the women who so desperately wanted to die now hold their heads up and call themselves business women.

Robert and I have a full life here in the States. We are the proud grandparents of Jordan, the most beautiful girl we know. She has been my girl since the day she was born and I was there to cut the cord.

Jordan and I always make a big deal of Christmas with a big winter wonderland scene that takes up half the living room. We staple—much to Robert's chagrin—icicle lights from the ceiling and hang a silver disco ball in the middle. There are Christmas trees, animated figures, and nutcrackers in our fantasy display.

We bake and decorate cookies and pass them out to our neighbors. We dress up in our Christmas dresses, force Robert into a suit and go see the Nutcracker ballet. We have an annual Christmas party and Santa shows up with gifts for the children. It is a great time.

One morning last Christmas, I woke early and sat in my big chair watching the twinkling lights and animated figures. I was thinking about the book Tom and I were writing and the blessed life I was living. *God. If I never get a book published or if I never do anything the world would consider to be great, it's okay with me. I may never be on Oprah, but I live in the best place in the world. I have been blessed with a wonderful life. A fabulous husband. Our daughter and granddaughter are the best girls in the world. My life couldn't be any better than it is right now.*

Feeling greatly satisfied I went to my computer. There was an email from Pastor Ruth. She sent her Christmas newsletter with pictures of the Christmas party she and Patsy put on for her chosen children of the streets. They had a meal and each received a new T-shirt. They played games and made the day so special for the boys.

I remembered Ruth telling me about being in town one year, and she said people were shopping as though the stores were giving it away. It occurred to Ruth, *Who is shopping for the widows and orphans?* She made up a flier asking shopkeepers to donate items and to "give your best as if Jesus were there to receive it."

I glanced into the living room at all the glitter and wondered why I didn't think about the orphans and the widows as I prepared for Christmas. I was so consumed with making sure all our traditions took place that I had forgotten about the poverty I had experienced while in Uganda less than a month ago.

I burst into tears just before Robert got up. He thought it was his fault and immediately asked, "What did I do?"

"Nothing! I just got an email from Pastor Ruth and she was talking about things Smile Africa Ministries is doing for the widows and orphans, and here we sit surrounded by all this abundance! Why do I live here? Why do I get more than I need to eat? Why don't I have to worry about being thrown to the street?" My wailing continued. "Look." I showed Robert the letter. "Here's a picture of the team who fixed up Evelyn's house and a picture of little Joseph who was rescued from the latrine. I feel so selfish with all my things, and I understand Ruth's prayer when she told God, '*God, forgive me for asking for more. You have already given me more than I deserve.*' What can I do? Why can't I be rich so I can give more? Why was I born here and not in a mud hut with no mattress, water or electricity?"

I thought about Ruth's vision for a retreat for pastor's wives—her idea to pamper women and to let them know how special they are. I wondered why we had to wait for her to finish buying land and build the buildings? *Why couldn't we have a little retreat in April? How about starting with a tea party to honor the faithful women within the churches and the community?* We could give them a nice lunch with pretty teacups and gift bags.

That night we went to Tom and Sarah's for a dinner party, and I shared my tea party idea with them. Some laughed. "Rachel. These people are starving and don't know how they are going to feed their children, and you want to have a tea party?"

Sarah's mom, Bonnie, was supportive and said she likes to collect cosmetic bags and fill them with combs, soap, shampoo, a wash cloth, toothbrush and toothpaste and other personal items. Why not put those in the gift bags?

Someone else suggested instead of gift bags why not gently used or new purses. Would the women like that? How about nail polish? People started picking up on the vision and my enthusiasm mounted.

Sarah misunderstood what I wanted to do and thought I wanted to hold a tea party in Arizona to raise money for Pastor Ruth. I started thinking... *Why not? But not just one tea party.* What if I put the word out and people all over the United States held tea parties and raised the money and items for the big tea party in Uganda?

The response was phenomenal! Purses loaded with personal items and money came pouring in. Some held very elaborate tea parties while others had casual get togethers. A church in Gisela, Arizona had a Valentine tea and the men wore frilly aprons as they served the women— even the pastor pitched in with the fun.

The Quilt Angels from Gilbert Arizona made 100 tote bags. Many gathered journals and pens to add to the gift purse/totes.

Team members hauled all these items to Uganda. We were expecting 150 women, but usually more show up than are invited so we planned for 200. We also bought garden hoes and orange tree seedlings for each guest.

What a day when the big tea party arrived. Pastor Ruth invited everybody and planned the program while our entire American team showed up to support and serve. We arrived at Smile Africa's land in time to help set up the tent and arrange chairs. We unpacked dishes and cups and garden hoes and set up the food service stations. Pat Sullivan revved up the crowd by playing "When the Saints Go Marching in" on his clarinet. The women jumped to their feet dancing and clapping and singing.

Ruth planned an enjoyable program with speakers talking about God's dream for their lives, hygiene practices, the AIDS epidemic and more, and then it was time to eat. What a charming sight as these women, dressed in their finest, were told to remain seated while we served them. Tom had a great time serving tea and teasing the women, knowing they had never been served by a man. Some of the Ugandan men who had come to watch followed the role set by our American men and pitched in to serve also. That was huge!

After a prayer of dismissal the women lined up to receive their gifts. Colleen and Stephanie bought rice and beans to add to the piles of gifts. We gave out 175 jam-packed purses, 175 garden hoes, 700 pounds of rice and beans and 350 orange tree seedlings. The women laughed and cried and laughed some more.

Watching those women walking away with all their gifts balanced atop their heads, I thanked God for allowing me to be a part of something so special. We were told that some walked for three days to attend the tea party. Many took the beans and planted a garden with their new hoes. Those women will never be the same. Neither will I.

Although the big tea party was for pastor's wives and women in ministry something else was going on all over the bush. We were taking thermoses of tea, donuts and purse gift bags and holding individual tea parties for the widows. We made it a special time as we arrived at each home and served the widow and presented her with a new purse filled with goodies. We gave food, cooking oil, flour and matches. We sat with each widow and shared God's love with her. While there we assessed each widow's needs, listing the most critical first. If it was a need we knew we would be able to fulfill quickly, we would make arrangements to come back with a mattress, bed or whatever was needed.

What joy to go from house to house listening to the stories as we served the tea. One of my favorites was Fatuma Achieng. Achieng means "sunshine" and what a delight she was. Pastor Ruth had sent me a picture of Fatuma holding a bottle of coke. I noticed her fingers were missing, and Ruth said leprosy had eaten away her fingers and toes. Her face was absolutely beautiful. I told Fatuma: "Pastor Ruth sent me a photo of you."

"Thank you for receiving my photograph."

"My friend Betsy is an artist and is making a drawing of you. When I return I will bring it to you."

"I hope I live that long. God is good. That is why you've come."

"We've brought gifts. Do you want them?"

Fatuma raised her hands and laughed. "Yes! God has given me those gifts. I can't refuse them. Will you come back before I die?"

"I'm coming back in June. Will you stay alive until then?"

"If you lived closer I would come to see you."

"If you lived closer I'd invite you to dinner."

"I couldn't leave my house for that long because thieves might break in while I'm away."

"What do you do to earn money?"

"I go to town and beg."

"Do people give you money when you beg?"

"Yes. At times they give me money."

"Mzungus?"

"Blacks and Mzungus. And an Indian."

I asked about her leprosy. She said she got leprosy when she was around twenty years old and the Mzungus from Britain saved her life by giving her twelve injections daily. She married a good man who did not fear getting leprosy. They had a good life and were married fifty years with her being his only wife.

"Shall we go get your gifts?"

"Heh!"

When she saw the large tote brimming with rice, beans, porridge, soap and other items she raised her hands in praise. Then came the mattress! She was overjoyed. "A person who cares about poor people. God knows that person."

"Are you going to celebrate the resurrection on Easter Sunday?"

"I pray at the mosque."

"I guess you won't be celebrating Easter then...."

One week later some of us were in a Muslim store purchasing supplies, and Fatuma walked in. I greeted her warmly and introduced her to my friends.

Colleen asked, "Does she know Jesus?"

"She's Muslim."

"Can we ask her if she wants to accept Jesus?"

I glanced at the fat, stern Muslim who owned the store. "Yes. But maybe not here."

As we left the store, it began to rain relentlessly so we invited Fatuma to our bus. Colleen could hardly wait to ask her if she wanted to know Jesus.

Fatuma answered: "No one wants to be near me because I had leprosy. Yet you come to my home. You bring me tea and gifts. I know it is Jesus in you that causes you to do these things. Yes. I want to know Him."

Cali at 110 years accepted Jesus when I first interviewed her. When we made a return visit, she told us her neighbor and daughter-in-law accepted Christ too. She clucked at the gifts we brought and kept saying, "How would I ever buy all these things? These people have brought me all these things and what shall I give them?"

We assured her we did not need anything. We just wanted to bless her with food and a few luxury items. We brought out the nail polish and painted her nails and toes and gave her a colorful headscarf and a new top. She posed for us and said, "If only my husband were alive to see me like this."

After several weeks of visiting widows in the bush and having private tea parties I felt like we were not seeing as many as I would like. Visiting one at a time was fun but we were only able to see about three per day. I wondered how it would be if we had neighborhood tea parties with each of our special widows hosting them at their homes.

Back in the States I started planning for our neighborhood teas, and with the help of a lot of people our new team collected more nail polish, lipstick, colorful headscarves, purses, packets of garden seeds and more.

We had begun setting some of the widows up in their own businesses, so we also brought charcoal roasters, manicure/pedicure kits, knitting supplies, and purses for them to sell.

When the new teams arrived in Uganda, we were not prepared for the joyfulness of the neighborhood teas. We learned quickly if we were expecting ten women we should prepare for at least twenty. Maybe thirty. We put the women in a circle and placed soapy basins of water in front of them, explaining that this was their spa day and they were to soak their feet while they sipped tea and munched on donuts. While they relished their tea, we shared the story of Jesus using a visual aid— the "evange-cube" which is put out by the Jesus Film people.

These women had never been served by anyone, and now white women and men were kneeling before them painting their fingernails, massaging their feet and whispering, "Unto You Jesus" and asking, "Is there anything you want me to pray about?"

We brought fuzzy foot massagers, and after soaking their feet we dried them off and massaged lotion into their feet and shins. We slid plastic bags over their feet and snuggled their feet into the vibrating foot massagers and watched their startled expressions go from shock to laughter. They joked, "I feel like I'm driving a motor car." Many have never ridden in a car let alone driven one.

We applied lipstick on the women and handed them colorful new headscarves. We walked around with a mirror so they could see how beautiful they looked—more looks of surprise as they stared at the image and then realized they were peering at themselves.

We gave them flip flops or shoes and at times were able to hand out clothing.Before handing out their final gifts of food and saucepans, we would pray for them and give them the opportunity to accept Christ. We would tell them: "We're not here to buy you. You get the gifts whether you accept Christ or not. We are here to tell you He has not forgotten you and He loves you very much. We are here to show you the same mercy Christ has shown us." Many responded and said "yes" to Jesus.

What is next for the widows of Uganda? More businesses to start up. The resource center for women is a project we want to see completed.

Teams will paint the building, tables, chairs and walls. We want murals on the walls depicting women in leadership roles and framed Scriptures encouraging widows.

The women's center will have a library filled with books for women and children as well as Women's Study Bibles. Here women will come to be taught to read, write and do simple arithmetic as well as to knit, crochet, and do cake decorating. Classes will be held in hygiene, basic health and nutrition, jobs skills and agriculture. There will be Bible classes, budgeting and record keeping. There will be medical outreaches.

No longer do we ask, "God, where are You? Why don't You hear their prayer?"

We now know He expects us to be the answer to someone's prayer. Once we know, we can not turn our backs. Now we are responsible for the starving, the hurting and the broken.

Do you want to know where God is? He is here. He is in the face of the little boy who is getting his first set of new clothes. The little girl sees Him in you when you hold out your hand and show her you care. The orphan whom you allow to call you "Daddy" when he has never known a dad sees God in your face. The mother hovering over her child dying of malaria knows God is here because you brought medicine so her child could live. The widow who wondered which day her life would end knows He is here. She knows He has not forgotten her, because He sent you. You came so a woman who lived to be 120 could feel what it is like to sleep on a mattress for the first time in her life. God healed you of cancer so a woman in the middle of the jungle could hear how much He loved her and could spend eternity with Him.

The father sees God standing next to you as you feed his starving child a meal and tell him there will be another tomorrow and the day after that. When you tell him that as long as you can help it, his child will not know hunger again.

He is there when the scared parents carry their wounded child and see the lights of the hospital you helped to build and wire for electricity.

He is there when the little girl stands before her classroom and announces she is going to become a doctor, a lawyer, a teacher or whatever else she dreams of doing because you sent her to school.

He is there when the teenage boy says, "I'm going to have one wife and I'm going to love and cherish her in the way God intended for her to be treated."

You heard the cries of the Savior when He called you to the trenches. You said, "Here am I. Send me," when God asked "Whom shall I send? And who will go for us?" (Isaiah 6:8)

God. Do You hear their prayer? Where are you?

I am right here where I have been all along.

References

1. Booth, William, 1996. *In Darkest England and the Way Out,* E-Text #475, 4.
2. Yaxley, Trevor with Carolyn Vanderwal. 2003. *William & Catherine: the Life and Legacy of the Booths, Founders of the Salvation Army.* Minnesota: Bethany House Publishers, 130.
3. Wikipedia, the free encyclopedia, http://en.wikipedia.org/wiki/Howard_Thurman, 2007
4. Yaxley, Trevor with Carolyn Vanderwal. 2003. *William & Catherine: the Life and Legacy of the Booths, Founders of the Salvation Army.* Minnesota: Bethany House Publishers, 63.
5. Brother Andrew. 2006. *God's Smuggler.* Michigan: Chosen Books.
6. Eldredge, John, 2001. *Wild at Heart,* Tennessee: Thomas Nelson, Inc., 141.
7. Hirschmann, Maria Anne, 1979. *Please don't Shoot! I'm Already Wounded,* Illinois: Tyndale House Publishers, 144.
8. Lucado, Max, 1996. *In the Grip of Grace,* Tennessee: W Publishing Group, 40.
9. Yaxley, Trevor with Carolyn Vanderwal. 2003. *William & Catherine: the Life and Legacy of the Booths, Founders of the Salvation Army.* Minnesota: Bethany House Publishers, 21-26.
10. Ten Boom, Corrie with Elizabeth and John Sherrill, 2006. *The Hiding Place,* Michigan: Chosen Books.